Fuller

A Fresh Look at Learning to Read

Making Speech Visible

How Constructing Words Can Help Children Organize Their Brains for Skillful Reading

Jeannine Herron, Ph.D.

Forewords by:

G. Reid Lyon, Ph.D.

Former Chief, Child Development and Behavior Branch
National Institutes of Health

Joseph Torgesen, Ph.D.

Director Emeritus, Florida Center for Reading Research

D1208416

Making Speech Visible
By Jeannine Herron

Photographs © 2011 by Jeannine Herron and Matt Herron.
Designed by Marcia Friedman
Illustrations and " Talking Shapes" by Mitchell Rose
Editorial assistance by Dawn Mann

Second Edition
© 2018 Jeannine Herron

ISBN 978-1-933945-16-3

 **Talking Fingers Publications**
San Rafael, California
www.talkingfingers.com

This book is dedicated to
all the children of the world
who are ready to learn to read.

Table of Contents

Foreword

have known Dr. Jeannine Herron for well over a decade and have always been a fan of her scientific work in the neuropsychology of reading development and reading difficulties. I learned over the years that Jeannine is one of the few scientists who can translate complex research findings into effective instructional solutions for kids who are learning to read or who are having a tough time learning to read. I saw this first hand when she initially contacted me at the NICHD. Jeannine discussed with me her ideas for building a technology-based, instructional reading program based upon the best scientific evidence that we had at that time in understanding how children learn to read, why some children have difficulties, and how we can help almost all children overcome reading difficulties.

As I listened to her and then reviewed the materials she had created, I was astonished. She had developed a unique and engaging software program that brought reading to life for emerging readers. She called the program *Read, Write & Type!* After our discussions, she submitted a proposal for a grant from the very competitive Small Business Innovative Research Program at the NIH to fully develop the program. As I had expected, Jeannine received the funding and developed the first technology-based reading program ever supported by the NIH. She was then, and continues to be, a true visionary and a strong advocate for children.

When I first read *Making Speech Visible,* I realized once again that she was leading the field in the development of new ways to look at reading instruction. On the basis of her experience as a neuroscientist and educator, Jeannine has again used current scientific research to propose a new idea: Children should first be taught to read through encoding (connecting speech to print) rather than decoding (connecting print to speech). Jeannine contextualizes her new instructional approach within a context that integrates perspectives from many reading researchers. If one is looking for dogma or ideology, this is not the book I would recommend.

> "Jeannine has again used current scientific research to propose a new idea: Children should first be taught to read through encoding (connecting speech to print) rather than decoding (connecting print to speech)."

In *Making Speech Visible,* Jeannine leads us on a fascinating journey through the brain at work as it takes on the job of learning how to read. She emphasizes helping youngsters recognize the separate sounds in the words they say and then use the letters to stand for those sounds. Her focus on encoding prior to decoding makes clear sense as she links this instructional strategy to how the brain develops systems to "pull the print off the page" and to comprehend what it is reading.

Jeannine does a masterful job of integrating neuroscience, the experience of learning to read, and the lives of real people to illustrate the agony of reading failure and the joy that comes when one has developed proficiency in reading—a joy that is only realized when children are provided effective instruction based on the most current research that is individualized to meet each youngster's needs. The beauty of her thinking—which is reflected throughout this book—is its focus on the fact that learning language and reading starts as soon as the child enters the world. While

> "Her focus on encoding prior to decoding makes clear sense as she links this instructional strategy to how the brain develops systems to 'pull the print off the page' and to comprehend what it is reading."

many will argue that this is far too young to introduce specific oral and written language concepts to kids, Jeannine provides clear examples of how this approach can be very helpful and fun for the children beginning their journey to literacy.

Once again, I applaud Jeannine for her scientifically driven insights and her ability to make research come alive in very practical ways that serve all children. She is a gift to our profession and to the youngsters who benefit from her experience and knowledge.

G. Reid Lyon, Ph.D.

Dr. G. Reid Lyon is a distinguished professor of education policy and leadership at Southern Methodist University, Dallas. He holds a joint appointment in the School of Brain and Behavior Sciences at the University of Texas at Dallas, where he is a distinguished scientist at the Center for Brain Health. From 1992 until 2005, Dr. Lyon served as a research psychologist and the Chief of the Child Development and Behavior Branch within the National Institute of Child Health and Human Development (NICHD) at the National Institutes of Health (NIH). He was responsible for the direction, development, and management of research programs in developmental and cognitive neuroscience, developmental psychology, behavioral pediatrics, reading development and disabilities, learning disabilities, early childhood development, and school readiness.

Foreword

After reading this delightful book, I cannot resist beginning this foreword with two learning-to-read stories of my own.

The first concerns my oldest grandson, Andrew, who was a kindergarten student in Redondo Beach, California, in 1998. When his family visited our home for Christmas that year, his father told me about an incident that had occurred just two weeks earlier, in the first week of December. Andrew's teacher was using a program called *Zoo-phonics* to help the students acquire beginning reading skills. Andrew had brought home a small "decodable" book to read to his parents, and he was doing a very fine job sounding out the words until he came to one of those "outlaw" words that does not follow regular letter-sound relationships. When he tried to sound it out, Andrew's father said to him, "You can't sound that word out—you just have to learn it." To which Andrew looked up and confidently replied, "That's because you don't know *Zoo-phonics!*"

This story is funny because that's a surprising (and overconfident) thing for a kindergartner to say to his father. The incident was also very gratifying to me as his grandfather because I realized that he already understood that there was a system he could use to help him identify words in print that he could not recognize. My experience as a reading scientist had taught me that the letters in words are the most reliable clue to the identity of words in text, and Andrew seemed to understand this while still in the first semester of kindergarten!

The second story concerns a boy I'll call Tom who was not as fortunate as Andrew, since he had a mild reading disability and had received holistic reading instruction in kindergarten and first grade that did not provide careful instruction in phonemic awareness and phonics. I knew his family from the church we attended, and one day his mother called me and said that Tom's school was requiring him to change schools next year because they did not have services for students with learning disabilities.

Tom was finishing his second year in first grade, and he still had not acquired basic reading skills. I asked him to read a simple first-grade text for me; he said "I can't read it—I don't know the words." When I asked him to sound out a few simple words, he knew beginning letter sounds, but could not go beyond the first sound in most simple words. His parents couldn't afford private tutoring, so I agreed to teach Tom that summer if they would bring him to my office. I was able to have about 30 one-hour sessions with Tom that summer, and in August, he was ready for second grade. He still needed to improve his reading fluency, but he could read as accurately as the average beginning second grader. He never again experienced significant reading problems, although he did need a bit of extra support for writing in fifth grade.

Both of these stories belong in this book. The first one belongs because it illustrates the sense of power over text that students acquire when they learn to use the alphabetic system to identify unknown words. This sense of power leads to confident readers who quickly learn to focus on meaning because they have mastered the "word identification" part of reading. The second story belongs because it illustrates how seriously reading growth can be impacted for "at-risk" students when they do not receive appropriate early instruction. It also shows how reading difficulties can be corrected if they are identified early enough.

In this book, Dr. Herron has done two important things. First, she has provided parents with an entertaining, readable, and motivating account of important findings from recent research on reading. I am sure that my own reaction to the book is colored by my friendship with Jeannine, but I found that the context of her own voyage of discovery was a very effective way to lead me through the scientific content of the book. Another advantage for parents is that she has focused on facts about early reading development that have direct implications for instruction, and then provided materials and suggestions to help them put those implications into practice with their own children!

> *"She has shown not only how the speech-to-print sequence of teaching beginning reading skills is consistent with both modern brain research and with the logical relationships between speech and reading, but also how it might enliven early reading instruction."*

The second thing that Dr. Herron has done in this book is to argue for a particular point of view about reading instruction that is not novel, but that is also not widely implemented in current reading programs for beginning readers. She has shown not only how the speech-to-print sequence of teaching beginning reading skills is consistent with both modern brain research and with the logical relationships between speech and reading, but also how it might enliven early reading instruction. This second focus of the book represents a contribution to the basic science of reading instruction, and I hope it will be the subject of systematic research in the coming years.

In sum, this is a book I would recommend to any parent or teacher of a young child who has not yet learned to read. It will teach them about the science of reading and reading instruction in a very helpful and hopeful way. It will also teach them about the joy of reading and the joy of discovery as told directly from the heart and life experiences of the author.

Joseph Torgesen, Ph.D.

Dr. Joseph Torgesen is the W. Russell and Eugenia Morcom Chair of Psychology and Education at Florida State University. He currently serves on the Board of Directors of the National Institute for Education Sciences and is widely recognized for his research on the prevention and remediation of reading difficulties.

Note to Readers

You will see letters embedded in pictures throughout this book. We call them **Talking Shapes.** You may copy the letters on pages 124 to 129, laminate them and use them to start a child on the road to reading.

T A L K I N G
S H A P E S

Letters were invented to make spoken words visible. There are 150,000 words in English. They are all spoken using only 40 sounds. Each sound is represented by a drawn shape or shapes we call letters. Letters are talking shapes.

Young children can build or draw any spoken word if they can identify its individual sounds and link the 40 sounds with their letter-shapes. These Talking Shapes are unique because they link each sound with a picture of an object that not only starts with that sound , but also resembles the SHAPE of the letter that represents that sound.

For example, children hear (and feel their mouth making) the sound "t" in the word CAT. They learn to associate the sound "t" with a tree, and visualize the shape of the tree with its trunk and outstretched branches. That image calls to mind the shape of the letter. Assembling these Talking Shapes enables children to construct any word they can say. For more information, see Chapter 10.

Part 1

Why Teach Children To Construct Words First?

We can, and we *must,* fix our reading crisis. It's been brewing since before Jeanne Chall wrote a book called *The Reading Crisis* twenty years ago. It's "our crisis" because it affects all of us. Generations of children who read poorly actually deplete the intelligence level of our nation.

In fourth-grade testing over the past twenty years, scores have not changed very much—an astonishing 34% read at a "below basic" level and another 33% fall into the "basic" category (which means that about two-thirds of our fourth graders are essentially non-readers). Only 25% read at the "proficient" level, with a mere 8% achieving "advanced" status. Something is terribly wrong.

America has a vital infrastructure that needs repairing. It's not bridges, or water supply, or energy, or war materials—those are all secondary to repairing the crumbling brains of our offspring. To solve the worldwide problems of the future, these brains will have to know how to read and write.

The way a child first learns to read will set up pathways in the brain that are either efficient or *not-so-efficient.* Instead of focusing on "interventions" (special instruction given *after* children start failing to read), we can turn our attention to "prevention" and teach those little four- and five-year-old brains to establish efficient pathways from the beginning.

Part 1 of this book discusses the reading crisis, the development of efficient reading pathways in the brain and why constructing words first before attempting to read (a speech-to-print approach) can help children become skilled readers. Part 2 suggests practical, hands-on ways to teach the speech-to-print approach.

Introduction

Is there really anything new to say on the subject of reading and reading difficulties? Indeed there is! Recent advances in medical imaging technology have, for the first time, made it possible to look at the brains of both skilled and dysfunctional readers while they're engaged in the act of reading and chart the strikingly different ways in which their brains work.

The most dramatic new discovery is that if dyslexic readers are given intensive, specialized tutoring and improve their reading skills, one can see that the brain literally changes its pattern of activity to read more efficiently. These new insights—which are based not on theories but on the actual brains of actual readers—have led to new ways of thinking about how to introduce children to the alphabet and to reading, and how to prevent reading difficulties—the subject of this book.

Reading is a relatively new human skill. People have been using some form of language to communicate verbally for about two million years, but reading and writing have only been around for a few thousand years. We don't know what early language sounded like, but whatever its form, it's pretty clear that language—and the human brain's capacity to organize and express it—changed and evolved over the eons to accommodate more and more complex conversations: Mothers found ways to tell their children how to keep out of trouble, and fathers found ways to brag about the hunt as the family gathered around the stew pot.

So it's not surprising that our children, the inheritors of that ancient legacy, are able by the age of three to ask for orange juice and tell us why they don't want to go to grandma's house today. They're born with brains that have pre-developed organizations of cells—sophisticated and elaborate connections—to deal with the complexities of speaking. Their brains start out structured to process speech efficiently—*but there is no similar pre-developed organization to process reading.*

Writing and reading are relatively new inventions in human evolution that answered a growing need to turn spoken communication into some kind of permanent record. For small tribes of hunter-gatherers, oral traditions and histories served well enough. But when people began to gather in larger numbers, grow crops, and trade, longer-lasting records of spoken words became necessary. Spoken sounds could not be recorded; they drifted away into the air. What could be devised to stand more permanently for a contract between traders? Pictures and marks on clay worked for a while, but were of limited usefulness because more and more pictures were needed to record bigger messages. This process was slow and cumbersome—a more efficient system was needed.

> **"**Aha! I only make a limited number of sounds with my mouth when I speak. I'll make a different mark to stand for each sound I make when I say a word!**"**

One can imagine some Sumerian only a few thousand years ago pondering this problem and saying, "Aha! I only make a limited number of sounds with my mouth when I speak. I'll make a different mark to stand for each sound I make when I say a word!" And the alphabet was born! It has taken a very short time to progress from marks in clay to ink on velum to Gutenberg type on paper to computer print-outs.

Why do we care that reading is a new human ability? Why is it important to know that the brain has not yet evolved a permanent filing system for storing the complex elements of reading and writing? It's important because, as the brain learns to read, it simply has to do its best at organizing the critical elements of reading for instant retrieval. For many children, this organization depends on the way reading is introduced to them. If the millions of neurons storing these critical elements aren't connected efficiently, reading can become very difficult.

Parents, caregivers, and teachers play a vital role when children start to become curious about letters and words on the page. There's a strong tendency for parents to teach their children the way they themselves learned. But some old methods—like the "sight-word" approach, which involves telling children to remember the appearance of words by pointing out that LOOK "has two eyes in the middle," CAMEL "has two humps in the middle" and so on—won't help them build the skills they need for competent reading.

> "There would seem to be something fundamentally human about the desire to communicate. Why not capitalize on this desire by beginning instruction on written language? Across evaluations of beginning reading programs, emphasis on writing activities is repeatedly shown to result in special gains in reading achievement."
>
> *Marilyn Adams*

Most books and teacher-training programs have abandoned the sight-word approach and now focus on teaching children to analyze the letters in words (print-to-speech) and link each letter to a sound (letter-to-sound). This is an improvement over the sight-word approach, but it's still not the best strategy for organizing the brain.

This book outlines a different approach: a speech-to-print, sound-to-letter approach. It will explain the importance of helping children recognize the separate sounds in words they say and then use letters to stand for those sounds. It will show clearly why constructing words first—before trying to read—is more likely to result in a brain organized efficiently for skillful reading. It includes easy instructions for providing a systematic speech-to-print introduction to the alphabet, and illustrative stories about schools and researchers that have used this approach.

Anecdotes sprinkled throughout these pages will reveal the author's personal experiences that led to this book. These stories are set off from the main text and reflect things that have been said to the author by various people over the years that have profoundly changed her ideas or strategies.

For many children, understanding how to use the alphabet happens in the space of a few short months. If you're a parent, helping your child down the road to literacy may be one of the most significant things the two of you ever do together. If you're a teacher, you already know the pleasure of watching the excitement a child feels when she discovers how to sound out and construct, (or decipher) new words independently.

Learning to read and write is a staggering accomplishment, second only to learning to speak and understand speech. Becoming literate is one of the most essential major learning experiences of modern life, and it's the most important skill children can learn to help them succeed and be happy in school and beyond. It's a valuable tool for personal expression, and a doorway to the wisdom that the brightest and most interesting members of the human tribe have written down since that early Sumerian first carved letters into clay.

> **"Reading can be learned only because of the brain's plastic design, and when reading takes place that individual brain is forever changed, both physiologically and intellectually."**
>
> *Maryanne Wolf*

Don't miss sharing this experience with a child! It can be fascinating for both of you. Take time and care to guide the process in a way that takes advantage of recent discoveries to prepare that wondrous little brain for a lifetime of joyful and effortless reading and writing.

Pilgrim's Rest, Mississippi, 1965

"First, I'm gonna learn to read and write. Then I'm goin' home to teach my daddy!"

She was sitting alone on one of the church benches, watching some other five-year-olds play with the rocking horse. As co-founder and program director of the Child Development Group of Mississippi, I was visiting one of our many Head Start projects stretched out across Mississippi that summer of '65. We had 5,000 children signed up in a frighteningly racist state. It was the very first Head Start project in the country.

I wondered why she wasn't joining in the play. As I sat down beside her, she smiled shyly, reaching over with curiosity to touch my blond hair.

"What do you want to do here at Head Start today?" I asked. She looked thoughtful for a moment, and then her dark face lit up with a huge smile.

"First, I'm gonna learn to read and write. Then I'm goin' home to teach my daddy!" There it was, right in my face: The enormity of our task, and the power and importance of literacy.

Chapter 1
For Joyful Reading

Too many children across America are having difficulty learning to read. But here's the good news: For most children, reading need never become difficult or frustrating. When the brain organizes reading efficiently, reading is fun!

For a young child, reading is a very complex process to master. The brain's amazing system of nerve cells and connecting fibers has to figure out how to organize this new information: where to store the different elements and how to connect them instantly. The child's first experiences with letters and words will dictate how his brain establishes neural networks that will become habitual pathways as his reading skills develop.

Fortunately, new technologies have allowed researchers to actually watch changes in the brain as children read. For the first time, they can see what happens when reading goes awry. These new insights suggest ways that parents, caregivers, and teachers can help children organize their brains for easy reading.

Research from many disciplines has established that children need to learn how to identify the separate sounds in words (phoneme awareness) and link those sounds to letters (phonics) as they start to read. This is how children learn the code that humans have devised for putting speech on paper: the alphabet. But educators still have widely different views about how this learning process should take place. Should children learn to memorize the visual appearance of words? Should they learn to link letters to sounds as they see words in a book, or should they first learn to link sounds to letters and build words themselves? Do they need to learn all the letter sounds before they make words, or can they start building words with just three or four letters? How should the whole process begin?

The most recent research suggests that we should change the first steps we use to introduce children to reading. As children start to learn about letters, this new information needs to be solidly linked to speech. Instead of memorizing the visual appearance of words, children need to become aware of the sounds their mouths make as they say words, and then link those sounds to letters. Before trying to "decode" words on paper, children can learn to assemble letter tiles or alphabet blocks to construct the words they say. This shift in attention from visual pattern analysis to the speech system could make a big difference in whether a child struggles to read or reads with ease.

This process of constructing words is called "encoding" because it involves translating what a child has already mastered so well–speech—into the code for speech that we call the alphabet. Most people don't think of the alphabet as a code, but that's exactly what it is: a code for making speech sounds visible. And it's a code that everyone needs to learn in order to read.

"Encoding" and "decoding" may seem like cumbersome words to use instead of "writing" and "reading." But the word "writing" calls to mind hours of learning how to express ideas in text. In the context of this book, the term "encoding" refers to the very early use of the alphabet code to con-

> *The child must be able to grasp the idea that the alphabet stands for sounds, and that the word he or she hears or speaks are the very same sounds assembled to form words. If a child can catch this seemingly simple idea, then writing becomes a logical process of putting down an order of sounds in visible form.*
>
> John Henry Martin

struct simple words, which can be done with magnetic letters, letter tiles, or a computer keyboard. It's a prelude to writing, and the most effective route to reading.

> ❝That direct instruction in alphabetic coding facilitates early reading acquisition is one of the most well-established conclusions in all of behavioral science.❞
>
> *Keith Stanovich*

The most common way to introduce children to the alphabet code is to link letters to sounds in order to decipher (or "decode") words on a page. Children are shown letters or clusters of letters and are told that those squiggles represent sounds or words. But starting with the squiggles is putting the cart before the horse: The brain will organize reading better if we reverse the process and link sounds to letters instead! This book will explain why that is true, and how you can help with that process.

A newborn's brain is already listening to sounds and trying to make sense of them. Very young children need to have lots of experience listening to spoken words, watching adults or siblings speak, and responding to the speech they hear by using their own voices. As the brain builds its capacity for speaking and understanding speech, it organizes a vast databank of word sounds, word meanings, and the complex motor commands involved in saying those words. These elements are so well organized that this information can be accessed instantly.

You can think of the left half of the newborn brain as a kind of mental closet, with two built-in "shelves" (areas of the brain) for storing important elements of communication: the ability to receive meaningful words (stored on the UNDERSTAND shelf) and the ability to express meaningful words (stored on the SAY shelf). Humans have been talking for so many thousands of years that our brains have evolved to set aside these two areas for these specific purposes, and these shelves automatically start piling up with vocabulary as babies learn new words. The more the better!

But since reading is a relatively new task in the evolutionary scheme of things, the brain doesn't have a built-in spot for storing reading-related knowledge; in other words, we're not born with a READ "shelf" in our mental closets. The brain does its best to store this new information, but it doesn't always organize it well. Sometimes—if the new information about reading requires a lot of pattern analysis, or is presented in a haphazard or confusing way or in the wrong order—critical elements needed for reading can be stored on the wrong shelves, or even across the hall.

The left half of the brain (the "closet") is for storing information about language, and the right half of the brain (the "pantry") is for storing data about other processes like recognizing spatial patterns, contours, configurations, and faces. So it's very inefficient to cross the "hall" (the fibers connecting the two halves of the brain) to search for information about reading. These READ words should be put in the closet, right next to the UNDERSTAND and SAY shelves. If a visual word is stored in the pantry instead, it may take a long time for the brain to "cross the hall" and connect it with the meaning or pronunciation of that word over in the closet. Think of it like looking for your socks: You have a better chance of quickly finding clean socks if you always pair them up and keep them in the same place than if you store them haphazardly all over the house.

Obviously, this "closet-and-pantry" metaphor is a vastly oversimplified way of describing how the brain works, but it helps illustrate why some children have difficulty reading: because the essential elements of reading aren't connected by efficient neural pathways.

Children are better prepared to read when they've had lots of experience with speaking: asking questions, listening, becoming familiar with books and stories, and learning new words. The richer their early language environment, the better!

Many children are exposed to letters and print on a page as early as age three—sometimes at home, sometimes in preschool or school settings, and frequently in all three environments. All too soon, adults are encouraging them to remember the visual appearance of words—the shapes or configurations.

A better alternative would be to play games with the sounds in words, or construct words together with alphabet blocks or Talking Shapes letter tiles. Children can even find letters on a keyboard and discover they can build words themselves.

Children will only learn to read and write once. You can be a part of these precious first steps and guide their learning in a way that will help them grow well-connected brains!

66 When neurons fire together, they wire together. 99
Donald Hebb

This book is for parents, caregivers, and teachers who want to help children from birth through their early growing years to develop the capacity to read easily and fluently. You'll learn how to build a strong foundation on the UNDERSTAND and SAY shelves as children learn to talk, ask questions, and process what you say. Then you can start helping them build reading skills in a way that will give their brains the best chance of efficiently organizing this new information about reading. If children's UNDERSTAND, SAY, and READ shelves are well-connected to each other in the language closet of the brain, they'll have a strong foundation for learning to read without frustration.

The brain is wider than the sky.
For, put them side by side,
The one the other will include
With ease, and you beside.

The brain is deeper than the sea,
For, hold them, blue to blue,
The one the other will absorb,
As sponges, buckets do.

The brain is just the weight of God,
For, lift them, pound for pound,
And they will differ, if they do,
As syllable from sound.

Emily Dickinson

Things people have
said to me that
Changed My Life

New Orleans, Louisiana, 1967

"If you're looking for a field of research, the brain and reading is the way to go."

We had left Mississippi in order to put our two children in better schools. We needed a respite from being active in the Civil Rights movement in the heart of segregation and Klan country. We wanted a safer place to live while we decided what might come next.

My husband Matt wanted to continue his photojournalism and documentary photography in the south. I enrolled in graduate school at Tulane University School of Medicine, and was trying to decide what to do with my interest in child development, reading, and the brain.

My department had a distinguished lecturer series and students were asked to suggest speakers. I had just read a fascinating paper in the journal *Brain* called "Disconnexion Syndromes in Animals and Man" by well-known neurologist Norman Geschwind. It was about various cases where interesting symptoms were caused by the two hemispheres of the brain failing to communicate. I submitted his name for the series. To my surprise, he was invited and he accepted! I cornered him in the hall after the lecture.

"I would like to talk to you about dyslexia," I said.

"I don't know much about it," he replied.

"Well, Dr. Samuel Orton had a theory that severe reading problems were due to a confusion between the two hemispheres of the brain, and that the visual information about words was somehow not communicating with the remembered meaning of the word. Do you think dyslexia might be a disconnection problem?"

"It could be," he said. "You should pursue it. If you're looking for a field of research, that's a perfect way to go. We're just beginning to learn about the specialization of the two hemispheres and how they become organized for different processing. Understanding the brain and how it relates to behavior will be the most exciting research in the next twenty years."

Dr. Geschwind went on to become known as the father of behavioral neurology, and was one of the foremost contributors to knowledge about disorders of language and dyslexia until his untimely death in 1984.

After that exchange, I made up my mind to learn about how the two hemispheres of the brain worked together to process and create language, both spoken and written.

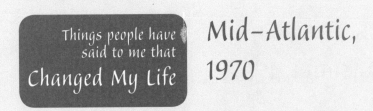

Mid–Atlantic, 1970

"Hey Mom! I can spell better when I type!"

We were sailing on port tack in the middle of the Atlantic, moving fairly smoothly toward landfall in the Azores. We were on our way from New Orleans to West Africa in our 31-foot sloop Aquarius. After some rough days, it was a relief to keep my food down and enjoy being at the helm.

Melissa, 11, was reading in the hammock, and Matthew, 13, was wedged in the companionway typing his log. I had been encouraging him to use our little portable typewriter, because he was left-handed and had considerable difficulty writing legibly. I was sympathetic because, as a fellow lefty, I could recall my own elementary-school tears over trying to write clearly. I remember forcing myself to turn the paper to the right and hold my hand under the line so I wouldn't smudge the ink.

Matthew used the "inverted" hand posture when he wrote, cocking his wrist and using the larger muscles of his wrist and arm rather than the fine motor coordination of his fingers. The letters ran together as if his mind was racing ahead of his fingers. He missed details like dotting i's and crossing t's. He didn't notice his spelling errors and could hardly read what he wrote.

He discovered typing on our voyage to Africa. For "schoolwork," we asked both children to keep a daily log of activities and events. We had a contract to write a book about the voyage with all four of us as authors. He soon realized that typing was going to make the task much easier. He could read what he wrote, for example. But realizing that he spelled better when he typed came as a sudden revelation.

On this particular day, he turned around with great excitement to announce his discovery. "Mom, I spell better when I type!" And it was true: Over the next few months, I compared several samples of his writing—both handwritten (in cursive and printing) and typed—and there was no question that he spelled better when he printed and typed than when he wrote in cursive.

A This is printing. I spell better this way. Also punctuation is better.

B This is script. It is faster but messier. I have been using printing a lot more lately. But I still prefer to type.

So began my interest in writing as an important element of language development, and in the possibilities of using the keyboard as a tool for facilitating reading, writing, and spelling in young learners.

Chapter 2

Watching the Brain Read

New brain-imaging technology now allows us to actually watch what the human brain does when it engages in reading. We can then compare the brain activity of skilled readers with that of those who struggle to read. The most exciting research to make use of these imaging techniques has shown that it's actually possible—with appropriate remedial teaching—to significantly improve reading skills and change the way poor readers' brains are organized to more nearly match the efficient neurological organization of skilled readers.

What follows is the story of a fictional child. His story represents the experiences of numerous students who have volunteered to participate in the recent brain studies that have changed the way we think about reading.

A Typical Day in a Brain Research Lab

The machine was familiar to her now, but it was still amazing to think that it could take a picture of her son's brain while he was reading. Johnny was lying down inside the machine, and she could hear him answering the doctor's questions.

Ann sat down to wait and thought about all that had happened in the last couple of months. Her son had been having a hard time in second grade. She knew she had to do something about it when he came home crying, saying that everyone else knew how to read, and he just didn't get it.

"I'm just stupid," he had sobbed. "I'm never going to learn how to read!"

His teacher told her that Johnny was quite bright, but that he did have trouble reading. She suggested that Ann look into the reading research project that was going on in the neuroscience department at the nearby university. At first Ann was skeptical that brain research would be of any help to Johnny, but she noticed that they were also providing special instruction. Luckily, she came to a decision that would change Johnny's life.

Eight weeks ago, when Ann and Johnny had agreed to be part of the study, the researchers tested his reading skills to see what problems he had. He did poorly at recognizing words, but what Dr. Matthews found most interesting was the fact that Johnny couldn't identify the separate sounds in words.

"When I say the word CAT, my mouth is making three sounds," Dr Matthews explained, "the sounds 'c,' 'a,' and 't.' What are the sounds in the word PIG?" Johnny couldn't tell him.

The first pictures of Johnny's brain had showed that he was activating mostly the right side of his brain when he did reading tasks. Dr. Matthews said that skilled readers used mostly the left side of their brains for these tasks.

"He's not using his brain efficiently for reading," he said. "We'd like to give him about 80 hours of special instruction and see whether his reading improves. Then we'll look at his brain again and see if there are any changes."

Johnny had faithfully come in for 2 hours every day for the last 8 weeks. The researchers taught him to pay attention to the way his mouth moved when he made the different sounds in words. He learned that the speech sounds he pronounced could be represented by letters. Finally he began to understand what reading was about. Yesterday, when they tested his reading, it had improved dramatically!

Ann stood up and went to the window. She was impatient for the brain imaging to be over. Today would be an interesting day: They would see whether

Johnny was using his brain differently to do the same reading tasks he had done 8 weeks ago.

When the new pictures were ready, Dr. Matthews was as anxious as Ann and Johnny were to look at them. He put them up beside the original pictures. The results were startling: Although Johnny had been using areas of his right hemisphere 8 weeks ago, now the right hemisphere's activity had diminished and he was clearly using areas in the left hemisphere. When Dr. Matthews put up a picture of a brain of a skilled reader, the activation showing in the left side of the brain was very similar to what they were seeing in Johnny's new pictures.

"Bingo!" he exclaimed. "Congratulations, Johnny—you're going to help us explain to the world how to help children learn to read!"

"But wait a minute!" Ann exploded. "If it took just 8 weeks to fix this and you literally changed his brain, how come he didn't learn to read this way in school? Why did his brain start working inefficiently in the first place? How should children be taught so that they don't start using the wrong side of their brains?"

"We don't know all the answers yet," Dr. Matthews replied. "Some children with severe reading problems (dyslexia) may have a genetic difference that affects how the brain organizes itself. However, we now think that many children labeled with reading disabilities may simply have had ineffective early instruction. It appears that some children are more vulnerable and need more intense instruction than others, and we don't know why. But it should be possible to teach the skills Johnny has just learned starting in kindergarten or even earlier. The children who find reading and writing easy should be allowed to tackle more and more challenging stories, and the children who need help should get more intense instruction until they are aware of the different sounds their mouths make when they say words and can link those sounds with letters."

He smiled. "Anyway, I think Johnny is on his way!"

The new brain-imaging techniques have changed the way we think about reading because they've shown that struggling readers are using inefficient brain pathways, mostly in the wrong half of the brain. The most dramatic discoveries, however, are exactly like what happened to Johnny: *Intense phonologically-based intervention significantly improved reading skills and changed the way the brain organized itself for reading!*

There are far too many Johnnies in America. Federal studies say that poor readers may number as many as 20 million children. More than one-third of fourth graders can't read simple books. These students grow into adults who can't read bus schedules or the labels on medicine bottles. Another 33% are very poor readers. What's the best way to deal with this problem? *It's to prevent reading difficulties from happening in the first place!*

"The U.S. Office of Technology has estimated that 25% of the adult work force does not read well enough to meet the requirements of today's workplace."

There's no longer any doubt that, in order to read successfully, children need to be aware of the sounds they make when they say words and know how those sounds are linked with letters. But the most important question is the one Ann asked: How should children be taught these skills so that they don't start using the wrong side of their brains?

There are four basic steps for building the neural networks for skilled reading:

- **First** comes speech. Children need to build a good foundation on the SAY and UNDERSTAND shelves—that means lots of conversations to develop a rich vocabulary and ways to ask questions, tell stories, pursue information, and make jokes.

- **Second,** children should learn to play with the sounds of words in songs, rhymes, and games like "pig Latin" so that they can easily identify the individual sounds they make as they pronounce words (this is called *phoneme awareness*). This helps them learn that their mouths move differently to make the various sounds.

- **Third,** they need to learn to link those sounds with the letters that represent them (phonics), and begin to construct regularly spelled words using all 40 sounds in English.

- **Fourth,** they should read the words they build, and develop habitual neural pathways that will give them the best chance of connecting READ to SAY and UNDERSTAND in the left brain's language closet.

These four easy steps are the most efficient and enjoyable way to develop phoneme awareness and learn the phonics code, the essential early skills for mastering reading.

San Francisco, California, 1975

"Let's use the EEG to study brain organization in dyslexics."

We were eating lunch at our favorite dim-sum restaurant not far from Langley Porter Psychiatric Institute. Robert Ornstein and David Galin had invited me to do a post-doc with them after I finished my Ph.D. research at Stanford Research Institute. I had been urging them to think about studying brain organization in dyslexics and we were heatedly discussing how we might do it.

"But first we have to be able to show that our EEG measures—electroencephalograph signals were the latest thing in brain-imaging technology at the time—can demonstrate a difference in brains that we already know are probably organized differently," David argued. "We know that most right-handers process language in the left hemisphere and spatial problems in the right, and that left-handers have a somewhat different pattern of organization."

"That's right," Bob agreed. "If we can use our EEG measure to show differences in the brains of left- and right-handers, then we can use it to look for possible differences in dyslexics."

That lunch was followed by a few years of studying EEG patterns in right-handers, left-handers, and ambidexters (people who can use both hands equally well). The technique seemed to work!: We successfully showed the expected differences in brain organization between these groups.

I then organized a conference about left-handedness, which I called The Sinistral Mind. The faculty who attended offered such interesting and diverse research that Academic Press asked me to edit a book titled *Neuropsychology of Left-Handedness*. One of the greatest thrills of my early career was to discover a three-page, very favorable review of the book in the journal *Science*.

We now knew something about how the organization of the brain differs with handedness. It was time to move on to dyslexia!

Chapter 3
The Closet and the Pantry

Let's take a peek at what your brain might look like in order to understand what was happening in Johnny's brain-imaging experiment (described in the last chapter).

This diagram shows what your brain would look like if you could peer down from above your head at the two halves of your brain. (That's your nose at the top and the back of your head is at the bottom.) The two halves (called "hemispheres") are a bit like the two halves of a walnut in a shell. They're connected by a large bundle of nerve fibers that pass information from one side to the other.

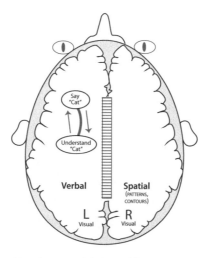

Figure 1. Major functions of the brain's left and right hemispheres.

Although the way your brain is organized is highly complex, it's easy to remember the location of a few important functions used in reading. The left half (which we called the "closet") is specialized for language in most people (except for some left-handers). The right half (which we called the "pantry") is specialized for recognizing faces, processing spatial concepts, and remembering or creating music. In general, the right side is better at recognizing contours and patterns.

Did anyone ever say to you, "He can't see the forest for the trees"? The right brain sees the big picture—"the forest." The left brain is better at dealing with details ("the trees") and sequencing pieces together.

At birth, your left brain closet was already organized with the SAY and UNDERSTAND shelves, which were ready to store new information about language.

The SAY shelf, devoted to speech, is located near the front of your left brain, close to a strip of nerve cells that are specialized for telling muscles what to do. (If you use your left hand to point to your left temple, that's about where this shelf is.) Speech is a very complex motor activity, so this shelf is like a huge database that gradually gets filled with the pronunciations of words: all the motor commands given to muscles to articulate those words, and the sensory feel of the muscles making those sounds.

The UNDERSTAND shelf, which deals with comprehension, is located farther back in your left brain, closer to your ear and to nerve cells that process incoming auditory information. (If you use your left hand to point to the top of your left ear, that's about where this shelf is.) This database stores the meanings of words: all the various ways they can be used to communicate ideas.

There's a large bundle of nerve fibers that connects these two areas. This connecting cable started out as a simple pathway when you were born, and grew to become more like a superhighway as you learned new words. By the time you were 3, these databases were probably already filled with 1,000–2,000 words.

Like most people, you probably process reading in your left brain in an area just behind the UNDERSTAND shelf, right between the auditory and visual areas of your brain (where you can utilize both auditory and visual information). In her book *Overcoming Dyslexia,* Dr. Sally Shaywitz called this spot the "word form" area; it's the area activated for skilled reading. In Figure 2, it's labeled READ "CAT."

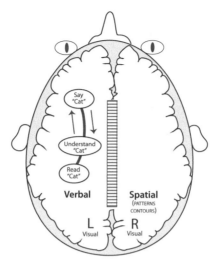

*Figure 2. The "word form" area—labeled "READ 'CAT'"—
located close to the speech and comprehension areas of the left hemisphere.*

So what was happening in Johnny's brain in the story of the brain-imaging experiment? This is where things gets very interesting!

What happened to the fictional Johnny was similar to what actually happened to eight dyslexics in research by G. Panagiotis Simos and his colleagues. (You can see the actual brain images by looking up research by Simos et al, 2002. Several other papers—such as Aylward, 2003—report similar results.) When Johnny's brain was first imaged, it looked something like the brain in Figure 3: There was strong activity in the right brain and very weak activity in the left brain.

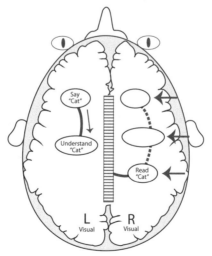

Figure 3. A dyslexic brain activating the right hemisphere to read instead of the left.

As you remember, the most exciting result was what happened after Johnny was given intense instruction (in phoneme awareness and phonics, with an emphasis on pronouncing the sounds in words) for 2 hours a day, 80 hours altogether: Johnny's reading improved dramatically and his brain activity shifted. The right hemisphere's activity diminished and the left hemisphere's activity markedly increased to look more like what's seen in skilled readers! (See Figure 4.)

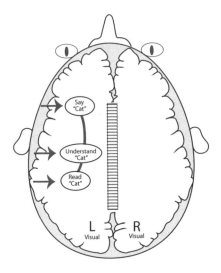

Figure 4. A skilled reader's brain. Pronunciation, meaning, and visual recognition of words are all in the left hemisphere.

What are the implications of these extraordinary studies? First of all, it seems clear that Johnny was trying to use the wrong hemisphere to read. The three components that he needed to connect for skilled reading—pronunciation, meaning, and visual appearance (what we called SAY, UNDERSTAND, and READ, respectively)—were not even in the same hemisphere!

But the good news is that intense intervention not only improved his reading but actually changed the way he used his brain! After intervention, all three components were most actively concentrated in the left hemisphere.

These studies suggest that the kind of instruction children receive as they're learning to read is extremely important, especially for children who may be vulnerable to reading difficulties. It seems clear that many children's reading difficulties might be prevented by providing them—from an early age—with instruction (like the intervention used above) that draws their attention to how they pronounce each sound in a word and systematically shows them how to associate those sounds with letters.

Researchers don't yet know why dyslexics tend to activate the right hemisphere when reading. There is evidence that some dyslexics may have an inherited difficulty with processing or remembering the sounds of speech, so visual strategies (which are processed in the right hemisphere) may become more appealing. Or they may have more difficulty than other children transferring information across those fibers that connect the two halves of the brain.

It's reasonable to suppose that some children might simply start with an inefficient strategy. Memorizing the appearance of words or trying to recognize visual patterns of letters may activate the right hemisphere, which is best at handling patterns and configurations. There is a great deal of evidence from patients who have suffered brain injuries that the right hemisphere is better than the left at pattern recognition, spatial analysis, contours, and "seeing the forest rather than the trees." So if children start out their reading by activating visual processing—trying to remember the appearance of letters or words—they may initially engage the right hemisphere for the job of pattern recognition.

Once the right hemisphere is primed in this way, it may continue to try to do the job of reading. While most children can easily pass information across the bundle of fibers that connect the two hemispheres, this cross-hemisphere processing might be more problematic for children at risk for reading difficulties. For these children, this connection might be less efficient, leading them to store and process more and more reading information in the right hemisphere, far from those SAY and UNDERSTAND areas that process speech and the meanings of words. The end result would be a pattern of activity in the right brain like Johnny's before his intervention.

This kind of brain research is still young, and there's still a great deal to learn about how the brain learns to read and why some children seem to be vulnerable to reading difficulties while others seem to learn without any instruction at all. Whatever the cause, why wait for intervention? In other words, why wait for Johnny to start to fail?

When a child like Johnny is first introduced to the alphabet, he can start by turning his own words into print. That way, when he encodes a word, his brain has already accessed the pronunciation and meaning *before* he begins the task of constructing it. However, if he begins with reading, he is confronted with a meaningless group of letters and has to struggle to figure out the pronunciation and then find the place in his brain where he has stored the meaning of that word.

The great Swiss psychologist Piaget wrote about how new information is assimilated into the existing cognitive structure of the brain. We associate new information with something we have already learned or experienced; that's how we remember. However, there is no pre-existing cognitive structure to help a child understand that a word on paper is a string of letters that stand for sounds. The only pre-existing network is speech. However, if a child can experience assembling letters together to represent the sounds his mouth is pronouncing, the whole idea of how words get on paper begins to make sense. The new information about reading is being connected to something he already knows.

Building words (called "encoding") is an easy and enjoyable way to begin the magical experience of teaching a child to read. Remember that encoding is an early form of writing—it doesn't necessarily mean drawing letters with a pencil or expressing thoughts and ideas in print. That can come a little later, along with reading. Encoding is simply a first step in mastering phoneme awareness and phonics, and it can be done with letter tiles or a keyboard even before those little fingers can draw letters with a pencil.

Things people have
said to me that
Changed My Life

UC San Francisco,
Langley Porter Institute, 1979

"Hurry up! My son is getting older and he still can't read!"

She had left Joe in the EEG lab with my fellow psychology researcher, who would be examining Joe's brainwaves. Now she knocked on my door and came into my office. I had enjoyed talking with this mom each time she had brought in her dyslexic son as a volunteer in our research. But this time she plopped down dispiritedly into a chair. "I'm getting discouraged, Jeannine. My son is getting older and he still can't read!" Those words would haunt me for a long time.

We were looking at every possible clue to determine how reading was organized in the brains of dyslexics. In 1979, it was still a mystery why some children had such difficulty learning to read, though there were many theories: it was a visual problem because they read things backwards; it was a vestibular problem because they had poor balance; or it could be a a difficulty with "mixed dominance." My colleagues—Robert Ornstein, David Galin, Charles Yingling—and I were looking at all the theories, and we hadn't proved any of them.

I was pursuing an exciting theory, suggested by the work of Samuel Orton and others, that dyslexics would have more mixed dominance than others—that is, that we would find that they used their right hemispheres more for verbal tasks, and would not be completely right-sided for hand, foot, eye and ear dominance. To my surprise, I had found no more evidence of mixed dominance among the dyslexics than among good readers.

We had selected only right-handers, so that if we found differences in brain organization in any of the subjects, it would not be due to left-handedness. We looked at eye dominance, ear dominance, and foot dominance, expecting to find that dyslexics would show a higher incidence of left-sided dominance. But there was no difference between the dyslexics and skilled readers even when we did the experiments twice with different sets of children. The skilled readers had just as much mixed dominance.

I had found convincing evidence of coordination problems in some of our dyslexic subjects, but tests that evaluated their sense of balance or nystagmus (the reflex response of their eyes to being spun around in a chair) did not indicate a vestibular dysfunction. However, I noticed that a significant number of the dyslexics adopted an interesting position for writing: They laid their left arms on the desk, resting their heads down on their arms, and positioned their paper way over to the right, so that their eyes were rotated far to the right as they wrote. I thought, "That's interesting. It looks like they're trying to put the visual input into the right-half field of vision in order to send that verbal information to the left hemisphere!" (The right half of visual space seen by both eyes is connected to the left hemisphere). I photographed all the subjects while they were writing. A significant number of the dyslexic students adopted that position quite unconsciously; the good readers did not. It was one of those tantalizing clues that didn't lead anywhere at the time. But now there is more evidence that they may have been trying to direct that visual information to the left hemisphere.

Skilled reader—normal head position

Dyslexic reader—slanted head position

But the most disappointing data came from the EEG: We didn't find any evidence of mixed dominance there, either. It looked like both dyslexics and skilled readers were using their brains similarly for reading and spatial tasks. Either our theory was wrong, or the EEG was just too crude a tool. (It would be another 20 years before magnetic imaging tools would start revealing the brain's secrets that were eluding us).

As I thought about what Joe's mom said, I realized that she was right—we weren't getting closer to any practical solution that would make reading and writing easier for her son. Little did I realize at the time that her words would change my direction and that I would soon leave the university to see if I could find more practical ways to help dyslexic children learn to read.

Chapter 4

Put Your Reading Where Your Mouth Is!

In addition to the new information from brain-imaging research, cognitive researchers have also done groundbreaking studies that shed light on how children become skilled readers. There is abundant new information about how the kind of instruction children receive can set the course for their reading future.

One remarkable discovery gives us a new understanding of how skilled readers can look at thousands of words and instantly recognize their meaning—an experience unfamiliar to an alarming number of youngsters who struggle to read.

How do skilled readers do it? According to research by Linnea Ehri, Ph.D., Distinguished Professor at the Graduate Center of the City University of New York, the sight of a word triggers its pronunciation, and it is this pronunciation that has been stored in memory for convenient access along with the meaning of the word. Our lips may not move when we read, but our brains are "talking."

Ehri writes, "Based on our findings, we have proposed that pronunciations of words are the anchors for written words in memory. Readers learn sight words by making connections between letters seen in spellings of words and sounds detected in the pronunciations already present in memory," (Ehri, 2002).

Trying to recognize thousands of words from their visual appearance alone (pattern recognition) is almost impossible. Instead, it's the "speech memory" that is the key. How do you remember a new telephone number as you walk to the phone? You say it to yourself. How do you decode and store a new word that you encounter as you're reading *Anna Karenina* or *Harry Potter?* You sound it out and pronounce it. It is the pronouncing that helps store a new word in the brain.

Storing information about words and connecting this information efficiently is a complex process. Your brain needs a good filing system for this enormous database. The pronunciation of words is stored in one location, the meaning of words in another, and the visual

> 66 *Children are wired for sound, but print is an optional accessory that must be painstakingly bolted on.* 99
>
> *Steven Pinker*

appearance of words in yet another. It's as if you need three reference books in the library, but they're all housed in different departments. They need to be close to each other for instant retrieval.

The brain-imaging work described earlier shows that children who struggle to read or are dyslexic use inefficient neural pathways (including areas in the wrong side of the brain) for connecting these three components. This breakthrough research suggests that using our "speech memory" for skilled reading works best if we originally learned to read by systematically laying down reading pathways in the brain that are closely connected to speech and comprehension areas in the left side of the brain.

> 66 *Our lips may not be moving when we read but our brains are talking.* 99

Research from other disciplines also supports this conclusion. Studies have shown that new readers must first understand that when we say words, our mouths make several different sounds. Each word is a string of separate articulations called *phonemes*.

We have become accustomed to saying that phonemes are *sounds*. But phonemes are actually more than sounds (although the root *phon* means "sound").

They are both motor events (articulation) and the sounds created by those events (pronunciations). This is a very important distinction because children can "listen" with their muscles as well as their ears. The muscle memory of saying the sounds is a very powerful way for the brain to manage the process of segmenting words into their separate sounds (phoneme awareness) and remembering the sequence of those sounds.

> **"**It is of little use to tell a child that a word is a string of letters that stand for the sounds in words. If, however, we can have a child see the visible assembly of a word out of letters moving to form that word, the idea becomes real, real enough for that child to 'make words' in the same manner—piecing them together a letter at a time.**"**
>
> *John Henry Martin*

The alphabet is a code for the pronunciations of words. It gives you a way of turning the sounds you say into letters on paper. Letters actually represent pronunciations, not merely sounds. Words on a page are simply speech made visible. *The alphabet is a code for speech,* and *speech* is the foundation of reading.

UC San Francisco, 1980

"Why don't you put on conferences like this to fund your research?"

We were having dinner after the conference. The University of California at San Francisco, where I was doing dyslexia research, had allowed me to set up a continuing-education conference about the relationship between the brain and behavior. Psychologists had paid several hundred dollars and filled a large hall to hear Drs. Kenneth Heilman and Norman Geschwind, two giants in neurology, give a full-day presentation of fascinating information about the two halves of the brain and their different specialties. More and more was being understood about how injuries or disconnections in the brain could change one's behavior and ability to learn.

However, for the most part, there was little exchange at most medical universities between the psychiatry department (where I was working) and the neurology department. Ken and Norman referred to themselves as "behavioral neurologists," but the term was not widely used, and very few used the term "neuropsychologist." The field was young and there were many psychologists and psychiatrists who were interested in learning more about the brain.

What I was doing in my research—looking at electrical signals from the brain to determine which half was active during specific tasks like reading—was definitely looking at brain-behavior relationships. I had one foot in brain research and the other foot in psychology. I longed to learn more, so I was eagerly asking questions during dinner and complaining about the difficulty of writing grant proposals and getting funded.

As we talked, Ken dropped a bombshell. He said, "Clinicians and researchers need information like what we've been presenting. Why don't you put on conferences like this to fund your research?"

It took me more than a year to process this suggestion. By then I had organized another very successful conference for UCSF, and I could see that there were many distinguished experts that people wanted to hear. When I finally saw, based on the results of our EEG research, that we were not going to discover the cause and cure for dyslexia, I began to consider more practical ways to help children learn to read. I would start a nonprofit research organization, California Neuropsychology Services (CNS), and fund it by putting on conferences that would provide valuable information for clinicians and educators (eventually more than 50 in major cities around the U.S.). In my own work, I would try to determine how computers (which were just being introduced into schools) could be used to address the problems of children who struggled to read and write.

Things people have
said to me that
Changed My Life

UC Berkeley, 1985

*"You should do a conference about how the brain changes—
all the myriad influences that effect our brains!"*

Through the conferences I was organizing, I had the opportunity to meet many of the pioneers of neuropsychology. One person whose work has had profound influence on the field was Marian Diamond, who showed that giving rats an enriched environment (by adding things like toys and exercise wheels) produced measurable changes in their brains—more dendrites and greater brain weight.

Her work convinced me that my instinct to make young children's environments rich with learning was the most productive way I could spend my life. Children aren't born with a given IQ—the kind of mental, physical, and emotional stimulation they're given by parents, siblings, teachers, and others has an enormous effect on how newborn brains develop.

Dr. Diamond found me during a coffee break at a meeting. "You should do a conference about how the brain changes—all the myriad influences that have an effect on our brains! I can help you design it and find the faculty." I was thrilled. It was a wonderful topic. We worked out a theme—The Ever-Changing Brain. Here is how the pamphlet described the program:

> The human brain continues to revise its structure, function, and
> chemistry throughout its lifetime—from development through
> maturation and aging. Further, this self-editing repeats itself across
> centuries, from the dawn of human history into the future—our
> brain activity changes culture and the environment, and they, in
> turn, change it.

At the conference, Bruce McEwen talked about how stress-induced secretion of adrenalin is beneficial for coping with stress in the short run, but can have harmful effects (including loss of brain cells) when stress is persistent over a long period. Fernando Nottebohm talked about how birds' hormones change the size of song areas in the birds' brains. Patricia Goldman-Rakic demonstrated the plasticity of the brain and how non-injured areas can take over for areas that have been damaged. Others spoke about the effects of toxins, drugs, and neurotransmitter imbalances that can lead to psychiatric and behavioral disorders. David Hubel described the work that won him the

UC Berkeley, 1985 (continued)

Nobel Prize—how important it is for the brain to get stimulation at critical moments in development, and how important the motor system is to the process of learning. The whole conference was such a rich environment that my brain was spinning!

We went sailing on the bay when the conference was over. Dr. Hubel was at the helm of our sloop as we left Sausalito. The wind was refreshing and the boat heeled over dramatically as we neared the Golden Gate. An ecstatic smile appeared on his face. "I've never done this before," he said. "This is marvelous!"

I came away from the conference excited and focused. My direction was clear: Children need an interesting and purposeful mental environment, and we, as adults in their environment, have an awesome responsibility to raise children in such a way that those little brains can develop to their greatest potential. How could I contribute? I could try to develop a system of reading instruction that would help young brains realize that potential.

Chapter 5

Conversations with Toddlers: Reading Starts with Speech

America has a crisis that rivals global warming, pollution, and dwindling energy and food supplies: Babies' brains are being wasted. Newborns have the potential to contribute immense creativity, innovation, and productivity to society. It is their intelligence that will find solutions to the global problems that we all face. But America invests far too little in developing that intelligence. Our society is, in fact, wasting it.

Educators who have spent their lives concerned with children have always believed that if only more dollars were invested in schools and in teacher training, it would be possible to truly leave no child behind and reduce the gap between the rich and the poor. However, *it appears that by the time children attend school, it may be too late to make a significant difference academically.* The human brain develops its faculties for language—and for using language to pursue natural curiosity and process information—in the first three years of life. So the most important period is when children are at home or daycare, *before* they attend school.

Researchers from many disciplines have clearly shown that the developing brain is profoundly influenced not only by a physically nurturing environment, but also by a *mentally* nurturing one. Babies' brains are designed to soak up language, and the critical period for this mental nourishment is in the first three years of life. A baby's brain literally doubles in size during that period. There is no other such amazing growth spurt in human development. A three-year-old burns glucose in her brain at twice the rate of a 20-year-old. By age 4, her brain size and weight is 90% of what it will be when she's 20. By age 5, she will know between 3,000 and 8,000 words.

Marian Diamond of UC Berkeley was the first to demonstrate that an enriched environment (as opposed to an impoverished one) significantly changes the brains of rats, making them heavier and creating more connections (synapses) between nerve cells. Martha Farah at the University of Pennsylvania found that "parental nurturance" (lots of attention and verbal interaction more typically supplied by middle- or upper-class families) stimulates the brain in a way that aids the development of memory skills.

"How can parents and teachers provide conditions that will most effectively promote growth and change in our children's nerve cells with their branching dendrites? Dendrites are like the trees of the mind, growing like poplars in the sun. How can parents help a child to develop his or her full potential and set a pathway of lifelong learning? Parents and teachers should create a climate for enchanted minds to obtain information, stimulate imagination, develop an atmosphere to enhance motivation and creativity and discover the value of a work ethic."

Marion Diamond

As long ago as 1995, Betty Hart and Todd Risley at the University of Kansas found huge disparities between the mental environments of poor and well-off children. These researchers painstakingly recorded and counted the verbal experience of 42 children once a month for two and a half years. By age 3, children whose parents were professionals had vocabularies of 1,100 words. Children whose parents were on welfare had vocabularies of less than half that—525 words.

Here's the important part: IQs correlated with vocabulary. Average IQ among professionals' children was 117; among welfare children, it was 79. The three-year-old children of professional parents had larger vocabularies than the *parents* of the welfare children! There are many factors that could contribute to this difference, but the researchers accounted for these statistically and concluded that *vocabulary was a major contributor to IQ.*

Interestingly, vocabulary depended on how many words parents spoke to the children. In professional homes, parents directed an average of 487 utterances—whether a single word or a lengthy comment—at their children each hour. In welfare homes, children heard 178 utterances per hour. The most profound difference was the number of "discouragements"—prohibitions and words of disapproval—a child heard compared to words of praise and approval. By age three, children of professionals had heard 500,000 encouragements and 80,000 discouragements. Welfare children, by contrast, had heard 75,000 encouragements and 200,000 discouragements. It was the *type* as well as the number of utterances that made the difference.

The researchers describe as "extra" all the times that parents used language that was about something other than controlling the child's behavior or daily routines. These "extras" became conversation, a give and take between parent and child. This give and take is important in learning to talk because the child's words prompt what the parent says. In return, what the parent says next will govern what the child says.

Babies are using the mirror neurons in their brains to soak up action information about how to respond to their environment. It's important for babies to watch your face as you talk, because they learn from watching your mouth and facial expressions—their mirror neurons are firing away, mimicking what they see.

It is the genius of this work by Hart and Risley that it shows us, without preaching, that attention and civil conversations with young children can result in a profound acceleration of the abilities that will underlie their future success in school, and indeed prepare their brains for using language for reasoning and critical thought for the rest of their lives.

> "There is clearly some genetic foundation that enables human beings to acquire language. But children must also have powerful learning mechanisms, particularly in order to learn the specific properties of their own language. Moreover, grown-ups seem designed to help babies learn."
>
> *Alison Gopnik*

So parents model what might be said in the language, and children practice choosing what they can say appropriately in reply. Passive language, like listening to radio or watching television, doesn't require that little brain to produce language, only to absorb it. It stands to reason that conversation is the most important stimulus for learning to think. Each new word broadens the scope of a child's understanding. Without the ability to communicate, children cannot ask questions, pursue their curiosity, or process the answers to their questions, and so they are less likely to broaden their knowledge or to develop and solidify social relationships.

The information about words and sentences they are storing helps them understand new experiences and can evoke associations with remembered experiences. Their constant question "why?" can drive parents crazy, but these little people aren't just demanding attention; they're feeding their hungry brains. If the response is "Not now!" or "Be quiet!" they not only lose an opportunity to practice language or consider a new idea, they also store away that expression of disapproval. They might not ask "why?" again so readily next time.

It is the give and take of conversation that fuels social relationships. As children display their skill with language, they draw more responses and compliments from adults and siblings, which in turn fuels their confidence and self-esteem. It's really fun for them to ask a question that a parent has difficulty answering; likewise, it makes a child feel powerful to make someone laugh.

> " By encouraging children's speech, by enhancing it and responding to it, by having exercises that encourage speech, by having them 'show and tell' with frequency, with an invitation to verbal complexity and sophistication, we avoid early problems that are based on insufficient opportunities to learn to speak. "
>
> *John Henry Martin*

By 19 months old, several of the more talkative children in Hart and Risley's study had heard or spoken 16 million words, the average children had about 10 million, and the less talkative children had 7 million. What a vast difference in experience! And the ability to talk multiplies as children grow. By 28 months, the talkative children had *31 million*—11 million more than the average children and 20 million more than the less talkative children.

If speech and conversation are so important in determining the way a young brain develops, the implications are obvious: It wouldn't be difficult to raise the intelligence level of our entire society, but we'd need to give more attention to younger children and their parents.

Pre-school programs are important, but they're not sufficient because they don't start early enough. The follow-up research on Head Start pre-school programs begun under the War on Poverty showed initial promise, but the academic gains were temporary: By kindergarten, children who had not attended pre-school programs had caught up with those who had. Although children in Head Start programs showed major improvements in language and cognitive performance, the primary benefits were that they adapted better to school and many stayed in school through high school. But the academic gains were a bit disappointing: By the third grade, the effects of Head Start had virtually disappeared, and there was little difference in academic performance between children who had taken part in it and those who had not. This research was later challenged by others who found stronger effects of Head Start, but the message remains: Younger children need this attention as well.

> *It wouldn't be difficult to raise the intelligence level of our entire society, but we'd need to give more attention to younger children and their parents.*

Clearly, family members and caregivers are the key. It is their efforts that will help young brains develop the early connections that will multiply their capacity for learning.

> *Clearly, family members and caregivers are the key. It is their efforts that will help young brains develop the early connections that will multiply their capacity for learning.*

Seniors can make a huge difference if they are offered the opportunity; there are millions of retired seniors who have an adequate income and would like something meaningful to do with the rest of their lives. Most seniors have many years left to make an enormous contribution to society with very little effort. They can certainly carry on conversations and read books to babies, for example. These elders—who have accumulated stories, experiences, and wisdom—can pass on this intelligence as potential energy for the next generation.

The more conversationalists the better! Everyone can participate in nurturing the next generations of readers, writers, thinkers, and doers—those who will protect the earth; resolve conflicts; develop sustainable food, water, and fuel; build innovative inventions; generate beauty, laughter, and entertainment; and teach integrity and compassion to the human tribe in the precarious years to come.

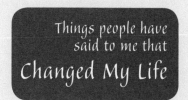

San Rafael, California, 1982

"You mean letters stand for the sounds in words? No one ever told me that."

As part of research being carried our by my nonprofit organization, California Neuropsychology Services, I was visiting schools to see what was being offered to students who were struggling to read. We wanted to see how children were being taught to read and how schools were using their new computers

I sat down with a fifth grader in the Reading Resource room. We exchanged a few words as she chose a book to read. She was obviously bright, but as she struggled to read a fairly simple passage, I could see how painful it was for her.

"What's that word", she asked, pointing to the word FANTASTIC.

"Sound it out," I replied.

"What do you mean?"

"Didn't anyone ever ask you to sound out a word before?" I asked.

"No…"

"Well," I said, "start with the first sound in the word. What is it?"

She was puzzled. "I don't know what you mean."

"Well, I would start with the first part, FAN. When I start to say FAN, I put my teeth on my lower lip and blow: fffff-an-tas-tic. The first sound I make is 'fff.' What letter stands for the sound 'fff'?"

"I really don't know. You mean letters stand for the sounds in words? No one ever told me that."

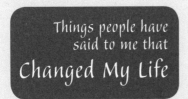
San Rafael, California, 1982

"We need better software. Why don't you develop something to help us teach our kids to read?"

I was observing in a second-grade classroom that had two Apple IIe computers. Jenny Robbins, the teacher, was excited about having the computers but didn't really know what to do with them. The school had only two pieces of software: a drawing program and a math drill-and-practice program. I could tell that Jenny was frustrated.

"I can see the potential of computers," she said, "but right now I just use them as a reward for good behavior. If the kids do their other work, they get to use the computer for ten minutes. But they're not really learning anything new."

"Do they do any writing on the computer?" I asked.

"Well, I tried that, but it takes so long for them to hunt for the right keys that they can do more writing when they use pencils."

"When do they learn to touch-type?"

"Oh, they don't take typing until high school. What my kids really need is to learn phonics, but my principal doesn't want me to teach phonics. There's a real backlash against phonics happening right now. We need new programs, Jeannine. Why don't you develop something to help us teach our kids to read?"

There it was: A challenge I had been considering, but not seriously—a way to get good phonics instruction in the door without too much notice. A good program could be a way into thousands of classrooms, but I didn't know anything about software development.

I began to think about how the computer could be used to teach the alphabet code. A code has to be used both ways. I had learned Morse code at sea—I had to learn to "send" as well as "receive"—so I understood the value of encoding (constructing words with the code), and I had some ideas about how typing instruction might actually be an added benefit. I knew that if kids were writing specific words, the computer could give them feedback about their errors. It could be truly individualized instruction! The more I thought about it, the more the idea gripped me.

San Rafael, California, 1982 (continued)

I talked to a lot of wonderful mentors, pioneers in the field of educational software—Joyce Hakansson, Leslie Grimm, Don Daglow, and others—and found my way around the software world. I began to wake up in the morning thinking about how the keyboard could be represented as two houses with interesting characters inside whose names started with the letters where they lived. The story began to take shape. But what should I call it?

San Rafael, California, 1982

"Why don't you call it Talking Fingers?"

My husband Matt and I have been soul-mates for over 50 years now. We have been true partners together, facing challenges like being active in the Civil Rights movement, embarking on a trip to Africa in a small boat, and writing a book about that trip. One of the best aspects of our partnership has been working out new ideas together; sometimes it was a story idea he was presenting to a magazine, sometimes it was some idea I was struggling with. We love this kind of exchange, and admire each other for the creative suggestions that spring from our brainstorming.

The best ideas come during our walks. On this particular morning, we were walking on the levee near our house. I was describing the software I wanted to develop, but I couldn't think of a good name for it. I was telling him about the keyboard houses and the fact that it was important for children to identify the sounds in a word, and then link those sounds not only to letters, but also to a particular movement of a finger on the keyboard.

"Do you think first graders can really learn to type?" he asked.

"Sure! It's going to be lots easier than remembering the shape of a letter and trying to draw it," I replied. "They can also learn to write with a pencil, but this will make their first attempts easier, especially for children who struggle with fine-motor coordination."

"Is there any other reason that typing is important?"

I thought about it for a minute. "They should think of each finger as the agent of making that sound visible," I said. "Their muscles will help them remember. We could even put little stickers with letters on their fingers. This finger says 'ffff.' I'm sure that the muscle memory of each finger-stroke is going to help them remember the letter code for that sound."

"What you're saying is that we talk to each other with our mouths and we talk to the computer with our fingers! Why don't you call it Talking Fingers?"

That was it! It was all making sense. I was hooked! I hugged him. *Talking Fingers* for the Apple IIe (the first version of *Read, Write & Type!)* was born! Later, when we formed a company to be eligible for Small Business Grants, we called the company Talking Fingers.

Chapter 6

Putting the Cart Behind the Horse—Where it Belongs!

Reading first? No, reading second!

The dramatic implication of the discoveries discussed so far is that *we teach phonics backwards*. We put the cart before the horse by showing children what letters *look like* and teaching them their names, and *then* telling them what speech sounds those letters stand for. In other words, we teach letter-to-sound associations rather than sound-to-letter associations. We start with the *visual* text rather than the spoken word, thereby activating *visual* areas of children's brains before *speech* areas. Reading should start with *speech*.

By the time children get to school, they are already very good at speaking and understanding speech. But, as discussed earlier, there is no pre-designed brain area for handling reading. When the brain is first presented with letters, it has to decide how to store their visual appearances

> **"**One of the most fundamental flaws found in almost all phonics programs, including traditional ones, is that they teach the [alphabet] code backwards. That is, they go from letter to sound instead of from sound to letter.**"**
>
> *Louisa Moats, 1998*

and patterns when they are clustered together to make words. As this new information comes in, the brain decides which shelves to store this complex new task on.

Obviously, this new information about words should be stored in a location closely connected to areas that are already packed with information about words—their pronunciations and their meanings—in order to build on what the brain already knows about words. That means starting by saying a word, segmenting it into its sounds, and using letters to represent each sound.

Creating a word with letters begins with the act of pronouncing the word, either mentally or aloud. For example, a child might say, "I want to write the word CAT." The meaning of the word CAT is automatically activated. Then each sound in the word CAT is pronounced in sequence as the appropriate letters are assembled. Once the spoken word becomes a visible word, then the word is read: "That word says CAT!"

When children use this process to encode words themselves, it becomes clear to them how the words in a book get created in the first place. As they master encoding, decoding begins to make sense; they understand why and how they need to use the code to decode (read) new words.

Pronouncing the word activates the networks already established for speech and comprehension. The brain then adds new visual connections (the appearance of letters and patterns of letters) to this existing foundation. Learning to construct words (encode) before attempting to read (decode) is more likely to connect the brain efficiently because it builds directly on the speech and comprehension information already stored in the left brain.

> **"**What is of use to a child interested in reading is explicit instruction in how the written language works—how it represents the sounds of speech, how it is produced with tools like pencils and chalk, how it signifies words and ideas.**"**
>
> *Sylvia Farnham-Diggory*

Consider for a moment what happens instead when the brain tries to *decode* the word CAT. *Visual areas in the brain are activated before there is even the thought of a word.* Then each letter is considered visually before its sound is associated with it. Finally the sounds are blended and the word is *pronounced*. The initial part of the task is visual pattern recognition and the very last part of the process is to try to access the *meaning* of the word.

SPEECH to PRINT (ENCODING)

1. I want to *write* the word CAT.

2. I already know its meaning.

3. I pronounce the word and segment the sounds.

4. What letter stands for the sounds "c", "a", and "t"?

5. I assemble C-A-T. I know that word is CAT.

PRINT to SPEECH (DECODING)

1. I want to *read* the word CAT.

2. I look at the letters. What sounds do they make?

3. I blend the sounds together. Does it sound like a word I know?

4. If I'm successful in pronouncing "cat,"
I will recognize the meaning of what I have said.

5. Oh! That word is CAT. (Meaning is finally achieved,
but only if all previous operations are done correctly.)

On the other hand, with *encoding,* the process starts with pronunciation and meaning. As a child starts using the alphabet code to build words, the brain forms synaptic connections between nerve cells responsible for pronunciation and meaning, then attaches visual recognition to those pathways. These early pathways establish the location and organization of brain areas that will handle the monumental task of reading. As the child starts using his knowledge of the alphabet code to encode and decode new words, these pathways become stronger. With repetition, these connections become an instant, accurate representation of each word. A neural network reflecting the word's pronunciation, meaning, and appearance is established. It's this well-established network that is activated for instant recognition of the word. In a well-ordered neural network, the essential "shelves" are all getting stored with reading information in the same "closet.

Dominican College, San Rafael, California, 1986

"I'm not going back until I have a copy of your software!"

Margaret Rechif walked into our computer lab at Dominican College with a resolute step. She had a deep suspicion of computers. She was a poet as well as a first-grade teacher, and she worried that computers would stifle creativity and curiosity in her students. However, she had been asked by the Walter Johnson Foundation to check us out and report to them whether she thought our projects were worth funding.

Kim Ford, program officer at the Johnson Foundation, had warned me about Marg. "She's tough and doesn't like computers. If you can win her over, I'm sure the Foundation will seriously consider your request."

Marg listened carefully as I explained why we had developed *Talking Fingers* and how it worked. She began to smile as she started using the program. When she was finished, she sat back and said, "I'm not going back until I have a copy of your software!

That was the beginning of an amazing collaboration that I will never forget. First, we got the funding. But the most extraordinary thing was that Marg went back to her school, Springer School in the Los Altos District, and talked all the teachers into pooling their classroom computers to create a "writing lab." After she had used *Talking Fingers* with her students, she taught other teachers how to use it, and finally the Los Altos School District wrote a successful proposal to the John S. and James L. Knight Foundation. All six elementary schools in the district pooled computers and created writing labs, and Marg became a "writing mentor" and circulated among the schools, showing teachers how to teach writing on the computer.

First graders started with *Talking Fingers* in January. Marg created paper versions of the keyboard "houses" so that students could practice typing words she dictated. She did warm-ups with the paper keyboards: The children sat on the floor and put the paper keyboards in front of them.

"OK, we're going to type the word CAT several times with a space in between each word. Everybody ready? Power up!" (They raised their hands in the air and plunged them down to place their middle fingers on the D and K keys). "OK, chant with me: 'c'-'a'-'t' space 'c'-'a'-'t' space!" She sounded out the word with them and circulated around the children, helping them find the right fingers. One day, when I was visiting, she was delayed getting to class. We found the first graders waiting, sitting on their haunches in the hall, chanting "'f'-'a'-'t' space 'c'-'a'-'t' space" as they typed on their paper keyboards! When she arrived, Marg looked sheepishly at me and said, "I have trouble getting them to go out to recess!"

As second graders, these students reviewed *Talking Fingers* in the fall but then concentrated more on using the correct fingers without looking at the keyboard. They used another program, called *Type to Learn,* as well for further typing practice. They also did more creative writing at the computers. I'll never forget one of Marg's lessons. She came in to a second-grade classroom carrying a big sack of shoes, which she dumped out on the table. There were huge hiking boots, delicate sandals, a pair of tiny pink ballet slippers, and many others.

She said, "All right, I want each one of you to pick a shoe." Children eagerly poked through the pile, chattering about their choices. "Today we're going to write a character description. I want you to think about what kind of a person would wear the shoe you chose. Is this person male or female? How tall? What does this person look like? What kind of work does this person do? What does this person like? Tell me everything you can think of about this person. Make up some really interesting characters!"

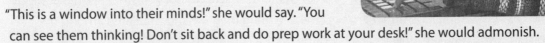

When the district got the grant, Marg gave classes like this at all six schools. She was passionate about telling teachers how they could offer "teachable moments" to individual students, circulating around the lab and reading what they were writing on their screens.

"This is a window into their minds!" she would say. "You can see them thinking! Don't sit back and do prep work at your desk!" she would admonish.

"Circulate! Compliment them on their stories! Be there at their shoulders to make editing comments. Is this in the right sequence? Would it be better to start a new paragraph here? It's so easy to make corrections on the computer and so much more valuable as a mini-lesson when they're engrossed in the process of writing!"

Most Los Altos students were typing fluently by the end of second grade, and the Los Altos District has consistently placed among the top five districts on fourth-grade language skills in California for the last 15 years.

Marg wrote the following as a report on the project:

"I Have Things I Wanna Say!"

by Margaret Rechif, Teacher, Springer Elementary School, Mountain View, CA, 1991

"When are we really going to type? I mean… I have things I wanna say!" said 7-year-old Mark.

On December 10th, 1990, it happened—and it was witnessed by a wide variety of people involved in bringing it about: Fifteen second graders were using their fingers to talk. They were writing fluidly on a word processor so that the circuit between thought, oral language, and written language was closed—allowing only seconds between the time the thought-impulse first fired in the brain and the time it took to produce a visual representation of it on the printed page. It wasn't magic—not even miraculous technology. The children were totally in charge of each step along the way. They did the planning and the thinking; they created the speech. They "changed" the speech into sounds in their heads so they could push the letters in sequence to form the print on the page. The computer simply helped put the letter on the page in short order to allow the author to hurry on to the next thought. They read back their stories to themselves and to each other. They made minor repairs, and then printed it up for others to read.

All I heard that day during their half-hour computer time was a busy hive of "speaking" 7-year-olds and stifled giggles. Each child was clearly focused on what s/he wanted most to say on paper.

Because they were being observed by visitors, the students had missed their regular recess for computer class. I told them to stop so that I could take them out for a special recess—obviously the favorite time for any 7-year-old.

They literally groaned when this command registered. The comments jammed up in the room: "But will we be able to do this tomorrow?" "I just live from Monday to Thursday for the computer class." And even, "I'd rather stay in and write my story than go to recess!"

It's not just the magic of electronics that excites them. In Mark's profound words, these children have things they want to say—yet their development often hampers them from being able to produce their thoughts in hard copy fast enough to suit their need to be heard and taken seriously.

Only 4 short weeks after starting our program, Cece began typing a tale revealing what was undoubtedly her innermost desire. With painted fingernails and an ever-so-slight smile, she wrote:

The Little Girl Who Wanted To Be a Rock Star

Once there was a little girl who wanted to be a Rock Star. But she was only 7 years old. Her name was Celia. She always pretended that she was a Rock Star.

When everyone was gone, her family had some cake. The next day she signed
up for jazz. She already could do the Roger Rabbit. And her teacher's name was
Kathy. Her best friends' names were Kim and Ruth. They went to jazz together.
By now the girl was 14. Now she could be a real Rock Star. And she lived happily
ever after.

Billy's story had five false beginnings. Without any prompting to revise, he used the toy-like quality of the computer to play with the beginning sentence. Finally, he settled on this:

The Rescue

One day at the beach, I heard my mom scream and I said, "Boy she's loud!" and
I put on my earmuffs. And she said, "A wave has washed away your father!"
And I started to scream too. Then I said, "Don't worry, I'll save Dad!" And I started
looking for my Dad in the sea. I swam three hundred miles south. I was almost
about to give up when I heard something. I sounded just like a concert under
the sea. So I swam to the bottom of the sea and I saw a man performing an
opera. I was my Dad! I couldn't believe my eyes—my dad performing an opera!
I swam just as fast as I could and I grabbed my Dad and my Dad and I swam
away back to the shore and when I got back the whole crowd was cheering.
"Billy! Billy!" And my father, my mother, and I lived happily ever after."

For the past 4 weeks, these second graders have been spending half an hour each day (Monday through Thursday) working at the computer, which I believe has helped them produce the fluid, written thought I saw on December 10th. They have been learning to type on a computer using a system that fully integrates the use of sound, speech, language, and meaning at every step. In the past 4 weeks, their fingers have been "in training" to automatically know which sound to retrieve from the keyboard. Without looking down and breaking into the "meaning channel" in their brain, their fingers are able to produce the sequence of sounds they want in order to say the things they want others to read. It's not hard to see why fluid thinking and total concentration were the result.

It seems as if it has been a very long journey to get these Springer second graders where they are today. From time to time, many of my colleagues and I have talked about a word-processing program that had the young child in mind—a program that allowed the computer to place the letter on the page in the correct formation, face it in the correct direction, and one that would force the child to move from left to right in a line straight across the page, from the top of the page to the bottom. Simultaneously, those of us who have guided older children through the writing process know that they become frustrated in the revision process of their writing, refusing to copy over anything that has been produced once. We somehow knew that a word processor would help them write their ideas once, and would allow them to "play" with the results until excellence was achieved. Secretly, we were all on the lookout for a child-centered word-processing program that worked toward furthering the writing process.

In January of 1990, I found it! It was *Talking Fingers*, a software program being developed in Marin by Jeannine Herron, Ph.D., the director of a nonprofit organization called California Neuropsychology Services. Almost instantly, I was captivated by the childlike quality of the characters in the program and the way in which the program used "sound associations" with the keyboard, as opposed to the usual letter association. The children were introduced to each sound through the characters who lived in the keyboard "houses." The characters either lived in Fadasa's house on the left or Jik's house on the right. This provided the students with a concrete way of retaining a visual image of the keyboard so their fingers could find their way around. I could see that their fingers would eventually be able to just "go" where they needed to, as if by magic, allowing them the chance to focus on the more challenging task of being able to put their ideas on paper.

The rest of the Springer School staff was likewise impressed and wanted to use *Talking Fingers* the following year. After several discussions, we began to think of our future lab as a writing lab—a place to use computers for the purpose of sharpening writing skills. We saw *Talking Fingers* working only if children could practice 30 minutes every day. This meant that we would need at least 15 computers to allow each half of the class to take turns using the lab daily.

We decided to begin using *Talking Fingers* with second graders only. With experience, I learned that the children all seemed to work best when initial "group readiness" work was done before each session on the computer—to orient the children to each character, to practice the keyboard together, to hear the stories together. Thus when the children came to the computer, they were highly motivated and interested in one another's progress as well as their own, and the characters had social meaning to them as well. They would talk about Fadasa (found on the F key) as if she were a member of the class, and Issa (the baby bird found on the I key) as if she somehow lived in their very own tree above the patio.

At each step, the children began blending sounds and then making words and forming sentences about the new characters they met—from "f' to "fa," and then to "fat" and to "fat cat" and finally to "Cass is a fat cat." Because of this well-developed sequence, the transition from keyboarding to writing is natural and the children make an easy transition from speaking to writing using the keyboard.

The children's success seemed to be partially dependent on keeping them paced at about the same rate instead of working in an isolated manner as is usual for computer work. The socialization of the characters in the program and the way in which it engages the children with one another seemed to add to the flurry of excitement of learning each new task.

Obviously, some second grade groups needed little practice, while some needed a great deal. This meant my role was to give each group sufficient time for becoming proficient keyboarders and to move them along rapidly enough to remain challenged. The software helped to do this, as well.

Anja, a perfectionist, was in a very rapidly-moving group. She wanted to keep up, but was reticent because she didn't like taking risks. She pressed very carefully on each key, sometimes causing it to register twice. For the first few days she was nearly in tears, so I adjusted her key-response speed, unbeknownst to her neighbors. The next day she was amazed by the results. "Look, I can do this perfectly now, Miss Rechif!" Immediately smiles and concentration produced greater motivation and progress.

Drew found any fine-motor task difficult, as did Julian. So it was not surprising that both children registered frustration initially when they tried to manipulate their fingers on the keyboard. Their fingers would become twisted and neither boy could remember where any of the characters lived. With added practice, individual attention, "talking through" each step, as well as spelling aloud with the characters and the sounds, both boys developed confidence on the keyboard. Julian is almost always the first one through now. Drew has caught on and keeps almost total focus for the 30 minutes he spends in the lab each day.

Initially, the motivation for all second graders centered on being given a chance to touch this electronic wonder—the computer—and by the fact that they had a disk with their name on it. "Oooh—it says my name: 'Hello Kristen.'" Eventually these same 7-year-olds became intrigued by the prizes they were awarded in the trophy room and by the fact that each of them got a different prize. Many would come into the lab mimicking the sounds made by the Trophy Machine as it doles out prizes.

As we have progressed in the program, I have begun to notice the motivation changing to a more intrinsic one for some children. These same 7-year-olds make up their own games, challenging each other: "Look—I can do this without even looking down. Watch!"

This internal motivation was to reach its peak on December 10, when the children actually began "really typing" their first stories, not by a hunt-and-peck method, but with all their fingers on the keyboard in the correct position. On that day, they began to see their own thoughts appear on a page in a form that resembled the way books looked after they were typeset and printed. The excitement and application of this new skill was to spread further when 7-year-old Christopher, who rarely finishes his work, ran up to me with a 3.5-inch disk in hand one day not long ago. "I've figured out where all the keys are that we haven't learned yet. I've been working at it on my own at home on my computer. Here's my book report!" Waving the disk, he continued, "It's on here. I want to come into the lab and work on it—can I—at lunch?"

What is true is that all second graders with whom I've worked seem to experience success on the computer keyboard as long as there was some lead-in time to practice skills they would then use on the computer. I was to learn, however, that first graders have so many "new" skills to learn that more time is required for them.

Our initial plan was to cut back on second-grade time and begin working in all of our first graders after the first month. The second graders balked vociferously (even viciously) as we began cutting back their time because suddenly they weren't given enough time to win a prize. And the first graders needed at least twice as much time getting started as the second graders had needed. So, after several very frustrating periods into the new plan, the schedule was scrapped and we went back to the drawing board.

Sometimes problems provide the way for even better things to happen. A new plan would enable me to see first graders as a whole class while leaving the computer lab open for first-grade parents to type the stories the first graders would "say" (dictate) to them. They seemed to need to see their thoughts transferred to print on the monitor and then see them again in hard copy. The parents helped provide this transitional step until such time as the children themselves could write their own stories on the computer.

Because I was in the classroom with the entire class, this allowed the classroom teacher to be trained at the same time I was training the children. I introduced the Talking Fingers characters using a wall chart. We made finger puppets and practiced our fingering on paper keyboards, saying the sounds as we did so. On several days, I brought in the computer and together we talked about the games and responded as a group using our paper keyboards. One day, when parents weren't using the lab, I disconnected the keyboards from the computers, took them into the classroom, and had the children practice on real keyboards.

The plan worked. In January, the second graders were proficient enough to be productive in a shorter amount of time and so it was felt that we could legitimately reduce their computer time. Our first graders had fewer things to think about and they could now concentrate on the mechanics of using the computer. They are thrilled with each new word they learn on the computer and talk incessantly about each new skill they practice. It won't be long until they too will be producing stories like the second graders did on December 10.

It's exciting. Mark's wish is coming true: These young children are talking with their fingers—they have "things they wanna say" and they are learning to say them with ease!

Sacramento, California, 1985

"We don't teach phonics in California!"

Kim Ford, program officer for the Walter Johnson Foundation, and I were driving to Sacramento for an appointment in the California Department of Education. We were scheduled to meet with the person in charge of technology instruction in California schools.

I was very excited about this appointment. Kim was interested in our work and in *Talking Fingers.* The foundation had given my research organization a grant to test it in the Los Altos School System. With Kim's encouragement, I was hopeful that the California Department of Education would take an interest in the program and help us get it into computer labs across the state.

We were prepared to explain the design of the program and the advantages it offered children. We brought our photos, literature, and floppy disks in order to demonstrate the software. I was still standing as the director arrived and asked why we had come. I enthusiastically began to describe *Talking Fingers* and explain why the program was called that.

"We talk to each other with our mouths and we 'talk' to the computer with our fingers. Each finger movement produces a letter on the screen that represents a speech sound. It's a natural way to learn phonics because children are sounding out the words as they write!" I said.

Her face changed. She frowned. "We don't teach phonics in California!" she declared.

I was so shocked I was almost speechless. I felt my face getting red as I attempted to explain why children needed to understand that letters represent speech sounds. She interrupted me brusquely. "You're wasting your time. If your software teaches phonics, I'm not even interested in looking at it. Thanks for coming."

That was it—the end of the meeting. I was embarrassed and inwardly enraged. Kim was upset as well, but fortunately the Johnson Foundation continued to fund our work, or all forward progress might have ended right there. Unfortunately for the State of California, the decision to exclude phonics was a prelude to an unprecedented decline in reading scores that was to put California almost at the bottom of all the states in national reading tests for a number of years.

Things people have
said to me that
Changed My Life

International Reading Association, 1984

"That fascist!"

I was attending a meeting of the International Reading Association. The speaker had been discussing Whole Language and the importance of teaching children to read whole words and to skip over the words they didn't know. The idea was to read to the end of the sentence, and then go back and try to guess from context what the skipped word might be. I asked him after the presentation whether it wouldn't be faster and more accurate to simply decode the word, rather than guessing at it. He asked me rather aggressively what I meant by "decoding." I said that children could use their knowledge of the sounds that letters represent to decode the word.

He snorted, "Oh, phonics is a waste of time. Everybody knows that."

I mentioned that I admired the work of Romalda Spalding, who wrote *The Writing Road to Reading*. The book had made an enormous impact on me because it laid out very clearly how writing was the best way to teach the alphabet code.

"That fascist!" he exclaimed. At first I thought he knew something sinister about her politics. Then it dawned on me that he was talking about phonics! I began to understand that he regarded Whole Language as the expression of freedom, creativity, and progressive thought, whereas he viewed phonics as rule-bound, overly-structured, and reactionary—the very opposite of freedom and creativity.

In the several years that followed, as I encountered scorn from teachers in California, it was odd to understand that phonics and Whole Language had polarized into political positions. In spite of the fact that I considered myself politically liberal, in the area of reading instruction I was pegged as a right-wing reactionary. But every once in a while a teacher would come up and, with her hand covering her mouth, whisper to me that she taught phonics behind the closed doors of her classroom.

To me, freedom came from being in command of the alphabet code. If you could decode and encode any word independently, that was not only freedom, that was power!

These experiences and the encounter in Sacramento only made me feel more strongly that I was going in the right direction!

Chapter 7

Marrying the Best of Phonics and Whole Language Instruction

Some of the controversy over the last 20 years about how to teach reading has arisen because researchers were looking at reading like the proverbial blind men looked at the elephant. You may remember the story: Each blind man felt a different part of the elephant and, since the elephant's tail felt different from its ears and its feet, each man drew a different conclusion about elephants. Likewise, researchers have looked at different stages in the process of learning to read. *Early* reading requires very particular skills of phoneme awareness and phonics that lead to success with decoding. Later passage-reading depends upon those initial decoding skills, but also requires adding different skills related to fluency and comprehension. Over the years, many researchers made assumptions that didn't take into account these different stages, and so drew erroneous conclusions about what the whole "elephant" of reading looked like.

A critical piece of information was missing. The brain needs to build the early pathways systematically by engaging speech and phonics processing. As these early neural pathways become stabilized, the process becomes more and more automatic.

> **"** *A critical piece of information was missing. The brain needs to build the early pathways systematically by engaging speech and phonics processing. As these early neural pathways become stabilized, the process becomes more and more automatic.* **"**

Now at last we have a way to understand the conflict between Whole Language and phonics that has so embroiled educators. Those who advocated the Whole Language method believed that children should learn to recognize entire words. They correctly observed that skilled readers recognize whole words instantly. It's obvious, they reasoned, that we grown-ups don't "sound-out" every word we read. It's more fun and should be faster, they argued, to read whole, meaningful words and get involved in the excitement of reading books right away. Skilled readers, they said, use the context of the sentences to make sense of the word, and this meaning drives them to continue reading.

What the Whole Language proponents didn't realize was that this instant recognition cannot rely solely on visual memory; it requires the memory of *pronunciations* as well. They didn't know that this *speech memory*—for letters, chunks of printed words (syllables) repeated over and over in many different words, and whole words—is the critical doorway to *meaning.* Each new, visual (printed) word must be systematically connected to language areas in the left brain as children "sound it out" using their knowledge of the alphabet code. As words and chunks of words become efficiently stored in this way, storing similar words gets easier. Eventually, the neural circuitry can efficiently provide instant access to all three components: *pronunciation, meaning,* and *visual recognition.*

And the process becomes the automatic instantaneous reading we associate with skilled readers.

How did this controversy about Whole Language versus phonics arise in the first place? In 1828, Noah Webster completed a monumental work: *The American Dictionary of the English Language.* This single publication standardized spelling for Americans and led to his teaching materials—*The Blue-Backed Speller* and *McGuffey Readers*—that were used for the next 100 years to teach reading to every child who attended school.

However, there were powerful and influential educators who questioned Webster's alphabetic, phonics-based approach. Horace Mann, John Dewey, and others promoted a different method that was based on word recognition or what later came to be called "look-say" or, even later, Whole Language. The *McGuffey Readers* were replaced in the 1930s by Dick and Jane books and, even though the new look-say method was unproven, it pervaded instructional materials and totally changed the way children were taught to read.

Dr. Rudolph Flesch loudly and clearly sounded the warning about the Whole Language method's flaws in 1955 with the publication of his book *Why Johnny Can't Read,* but it wasn't until the early '60s that federal studies began to reveal that an alarming number of children were not learning to read. Dr. Flesch not only identified the problem, he offered a solution: "Teach children the sounds of English and how they are spelled. Then they can sound out each word…and read it off the page…"

But by then, the Whole Language method was firmly entrenched. Learning to read was considered a process that would evolve naturally. Children were given limited lists of common words to memorize, and they added new lists to this vocabulary in each new grade. But increasing numbers of students fell behind. Remedial reading became a new industry.

> **"**If a child isn't taught the sounds of the letters, then he has absolutely nothing to go by when he tries to read a word. All he can do is guess. **"**
>
> *Rudolph Flesch*

In the late 1800s, not much federal data was kept on students' academic performance. But the government *did* monitor the progress of minority students, and these studies give us some data to reveal the results of the change to "look-say." In 1890, 49.2% of African-American students could read. During the subsequent 40 years, when these children were learning phonics from the *Blue-Backed Speller* and *McGuffey Readers,* this number improved dramatically: In 1930, 83.6% of them could read! Then Whole Language (called "look-say" at the time) entered the picture. By 2000, the Nation's Report Card showed that 45% of black Americans and 43% of Hispanic students were reading below basic skill levels.

America's reading problem has become pervasive and affects large numbers of individuals, regardless of race.

Twenty-five years after the publication of his first book, Dr. Flesch offered a second warning with *Why Johnny Still Can't Read,* in which he summarized numerous studies showing why a phonics-based approach worked better. Researchers like Jeanne Chall and Marilyn Jager Adams cited convincing evidence that Whole Language was failing our students, and that a phonics-based approach was the solution. But by then, the sides had become polarized.

What became known as the Reading Wars should never have become a political issue. But somehow, in both America and Great Britain, Whole Language instruction became equated with freedom, creativity, and individual rights, and phonics-based instruction became equated with lock-step, structured, follow-the-rules conservatism. Liberals and progressives flocked to the Whole Language camp to stand up for the right of teachers to teach as they saw fit.

> *Millions of students unnecessarily remain illiterate because the new method introduced years ago ("look–say") remains embedded in our schools in 2004.*
>
> *Robert W. Sweet, Jr.*

One argument marshaled to counter phonics was that every child learns differently, so teachers should be ready to employ different strategies with different children. Therefore, the reasoning went, if Johnny has difficulty with phoneme awareness, Johnny is not an "auditory learner". It's not appropriate to try to teach him phonics, because phonics involves auditory learning. This sounds very democratic, like saying, "Liberation for visual learners! Visual learners have their rights!" But it's a serious mistake in terms of what happens in the brain. For children's brains to develop the pathways required for skilled reading, so-called "visual learners" need phoneme awareness and phonics just as much as—or even more than—other children.

Another argument was that learning phonics is going "back to basics." Critics said that phonics involves boring drills and practice, and that it kills the fun of reading. Some teachers assumed that children must drill on letter-sound associations before they can get to the pleasure of reading books, and that was viewed as stifling and unfair. They asked, "Why should Johnny have to memorize all the letter-sound associations before introducing him to words? Why put off the fun of reading when he can start right away by memorizing what words look like?"

In the '90s, as researchers (and soon, publishers) began to realize the importance of phoneme awareness and phonics, they began to prepare classroom materials for teaching these skills. Unfortunately, with the focus still on developing *decoding* rather than *encoding* skills, these materials began to look very much like the old drill-and-practice, back-to-basics worksheets that certainly *were* boring.

Students were and still are required to do activities like examining lists of words and underlining all the consonant blends or consonant digraphs. They were asked to examine lists of words and count the number of phonemes in each word. Teachers were required to carry out scripted activities for several language-arts hours every morning, but very few minutes of those hours were devoted to systematically encoding dictated words or writing their own words. The pendulum had finally swung toward systematic phonics instruction, but sometimes both teachers and students felt regimented. Children who came to school already knowing how to read were bored by the end of first grade.

Happily, there is a simple solution that can resolve the controversy and bring peace to the classroom. Developing phoneme awareness and learning the alphabet code *doesn't* have to happen through boring drill-and-practice exercises. It's time to shift our focus from getting children to read someone else's words and instead teach them to *construct their own words first*. Both children and teachers would find that phoneme awareness and phonics would come naturally, be fun, and lead to successful, independent reading—a perfect marriage of the best of both worlds! Learning phonics systematically wouldn't be boring; children would be absorbed in the meaning of words (like the Whole Language proponents advocated), and they'd have the toolkits they need to write their own ideas and stories.

Learning to read by encoding is much more efficient. There's no need for Johnny to learn how to count phonemes if he's busy constructing words like FANTASTIC. Why count phonemes when he has to pronounce the word and identify the phonemes in order to represent them with letters? And there's no need for him to underline consonant digraphs like CH or SH if he's learning to encode words like CHICK or SHIP; he simply has to learn that the sound "ch" is represented by the two letters (digraph) CH.

There's no need for Johnny to spend time underlining blends if he's busy building words like BLEND; he has to feel his mouth pronouncing "bl" and find the letters for the sounds "b" and "l."

Why should Johnny spend time looking at boring lists of unrelated words and doing visual recognition tasks searching for blends when he should be storing that blend in his neural networks based on its pronunciation? Instead, parents and teachers can suggest words for children to construct from alphabet tiles, write on magic slates, or type on computers, eliminating the need for worksheets.

> "Why should Johnny spend time looking at boring lists of unrelated words and doing visual recognition tasks searching for digraphs when he should be storing that blend in his neural networks based on its pronunciation?"

It's a good idea for Johnny to start out by writing simple, regularly spelled words. The learning process works more efficiently if he starts with a few letters and constructs simple consonant-vowel-consonant words like CAT. That way, his brain can build up a repertoire of sound-letter associations slowly and systematically because with words like CAT, HAT, FAT, SAT, he is reactivating the same circuits enough times for them to become permanent neural networks.

If he tries too many long, irregular words (like JOHNNY) right off the bat, he'll be confused: "Why are there so many new letters? I don't know those letters yet. Why is there an H? Why are there two N's? Why is there a Y instead of EE? Why isn't it JONEE?" If he wants to write his name or another complicated word, capitalize on that motivation and help him construct that word. If it's a word he is going to use frequently, like his name, by all means, help him learn that word—its sounds and its letters. Don't try to explain why it's spelled that way, just help him learn it, and return as soon as you can to the systematic introduction of letters with regularly spelled words suggested in Part 2.

Young children are so excited about learning how to build words that they are generally quite happy to try the words you suggest. As soon as they hear a word, they know its meaning. They pronounce it, either in their heads or aloud, activating the speech and comprehension areas of the left side of the brain. Then they sound the word out, one sound at a time, associating each sound with the letter that represents it, tying this process closely to speech networks in the brain. This process is fun, active, and creative.

The dictated words can start with simple consonant-vowel-consonant words like CAT and HAT. Then you can start to systematically include different letters in these words so they become silly phrases or words in a story. Children *love* to learn how to write words themselves. Far from being a boring, overly-structured, drill-and-kill process, it can be exciting and engrossing. Realizing they can read the words they write can be a process of discovery. Learning phonics by creating words is the essence of Piaget's constructivism that is at the heart of progressive education.

> **"** *Children should be allowed to do their own experimenting...in order for a child to understand something he must construct it himself, he must reinvent it.* **"**
>
> *Jean Piaget*

Educational strategies should be inspired by scientific research, not by political proclivities. Every child should have the right to instruction that will organize his or her brain for skilled reading. If it's taught well, there's no need for phonics instruction to be boring; we just need to be sure that the horse is pulling the cart.

Early reading requires storing the pronunciation, meaning, *and* appearance of words in the left hemisphere. The best way for children to do this is to learn phoneme awareness and phonics so they can decode new words independently, and recognize most of the words in a sentence without having to sound them out.

We've already learned that encoding is the most efficient route to decoding. But decoding isn't the end of the story—it leads to the later-developing fluency skills. As a child starts reading longer phrases, sentences, and passages, his brain develops new strategies that rely on monitoring the meaning of the text, keeping track of the context, and making predictions about what's coming next.

Clearly, children need the best of Mr. Phonics and Miss Whole Language. Hopefully this marriage will be a peaceful one, and both sides will understand and respect the union!

"We're going to have to do it ourselves. I can fund it."

Leslie Grimm and I were walking out of the Broderbund building. Tears filled my eyes and I was overcome with frustration. It was obvious this process wasn't working.

Leslie, a brilliant software designer and one of the founders of the Learning Company, had already developed fifteen very successful children's programs, including the famous *Reader Rabbit,* but she was also frustrated. Computers had outgrown *Talking Fingers.* Apple IIes were rapidly becoming a thing of the past. Leslie and I had been trying to collaborate with Broderbund to build a CD version of my Apple IIe *Talking Fingers.*

Leslie loved the program and was as convinced as I was that it would help children learn to read and write. I was delighted with her assistance and ideas; she had given me invaluable advice on the Apple IIe version. But we couldn't seem to communicate our vision to the folks at Broderbund. We had been working with them for almost 3 months, but the results were disappointing to both of us. Educational software in the early '90s was known as "edu-tainment." Broderbund was big on the "tainment" part, while Leslie and I were focused on the "edu" aspects.

"They don't understand how to build this software, Jeannine. We have to keep the pedagogy of *Talking Fingers.* We're going to have to do it ourselves. I can fund it."

At first I didn't understand what she was saying. The notion was so inconceivable—do it ourselves? Wouldn't it cost several hundred thousand dollars? How would we create the graphics, sounds, and animations on our own? What was she talking about?

"I want to help you get this software developed, Jeannine. I have some money. We can put together a team of freelancers. Let's just do it ourselves, exactly how we envision it."

That afternoon began a remarkable collaboration that spanned 2 years. Leslie invested over $650,000 of her personal savings. For Leslie, her partner Jeremy Geuting, and I, it was a labor of love. They were 2 lean years, with no salary for any of us, but it was such a rich and exciting experience! For me, it was a dream come true. Without Leslie, *Read, Write & Type!* would never have been born.

Fremont, California, 1993

"There just isn't enough computer time."

"There just isn't enough computer time, Jeannine. We have a lab with 25 computers, but I have to be fair to all the classes. I'd love to get the first graders to computers more than 30 minutes a week, but then I would be taking time away from other students."

It was a refrain I was hearing from many schools that were interested in *Read, Write & Type!* Our experience with the Apple IIe computers in Los Altos, San Jose, and other Bay Area cities was that the first graders benefited most from three sessions at the computer each week. They not only learned the phoneme awareness and phonics skills they needed for writing and reading, but it was also an enormous advantage for them to enter second grade with typing skills. But Apple IIes were being replaced and the new computers were expensive. It was a quandary; 30 minutes a week was simply not enough.

What schools really needed was a cart of 25 laptop computers that could move from one first-grade class to another. But this was way before such carts existed. How could we build such a system in order to prove how well it would work?

Laptops were fragile; they would have to be protected during the transfer from one class to another. We designed what we called the Writing Wagon Project, with three Flexible Flyer red wagons that could each hold eight computers in briefcases. To our delight, the John S. and James L. Knight Foundation, pleased with our success in Los Altos, decided to fund the project.

We delivered laptop computers for 56 hours (2 hours a week for 8 months) to 94 first graders at Millard School in Fremont, California. These 6- and 7-year-olds worked with *Read, Write & Type!*, using eyes, ears, mouths, and fingers as they sounded out and typed hundreds of words, phrases, sentences, and stories. They did 10 minutes of the "warm-ups" devised by Margaret Rechif in Los Altos before settling down to the computers. Students also learned to use a word processor to type dictated words and write their own words, sentences, paragraphs, and stories.

By the end of first grade, they could touch-type and were competent with basic computer skills: They could boot the computer, access a program, find a file, enter text, do editing operations, save a file, and exit a program.

The 94 Millard first graders and a comparison group of 50 first graders at a nearby school were tested at the beginning and at the end of the project with the following tests: Blending

Phonemes, Reading Nonwords, Reading Words, Elision, and Spelling. They were also tested at the end of the project with the following tests: Woodcock-Johnson Word Attack, Woodcock-Johnson Word Identification, Wide Range Achievement Test, Spelling, and Typing.

Although the comparison group started out ahead on every test, the group using *Read, Write & Type!* scored significantly higher on Blending Phonemes, Reading Nonwords, and Spelling at the end of the project and made significantly greater improvement on all tests than the comparison group. They could type with the keyboard covered from view with an average of 93% accuracy.

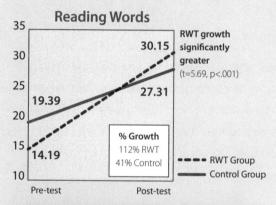

Reading Words

- 30.15
- 27.31
- 19.39
- 14.19

RWT growth significantly greater (t=5.69, p<.001)

% Growth
112% RWT
41% Control

- - - RWT Group
——— Control Group

Pre-test   Post-test

Reading Non-Words

- 19.70
- 14.94
- 16.75
- 11.95

RWT scores significantly higher (t=1.775, p<.05)

RWT growth significantly greater (t=5.56, p<.001)

% Growth
62% RWT
12% Control

- - - RWT Group
——— Control Group

Pre-test   Post-test

Blending Phonemes

- 23.96
- 20.66
- 21.50
- 17.61

RWT scores significantly higher (t=3.616, p<.001)

RWT growth significantly greater (t=6.34, p<.001)

% Growth
36% RWT
22% Control

- - - RWT Group
——— Control Group

Pre-test   Post-test

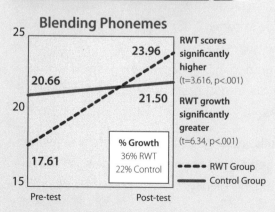

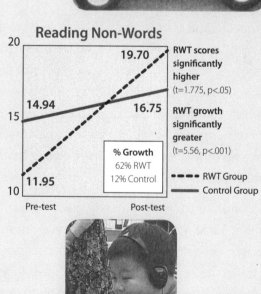

San Jose, California, 1990

"I think our parents could learn from this program!"

The principal at Hillsdale Elementary School was eager to help the families in the community surrounding her school. She was very pleased with what students were doing in the computer lab, and one day she said, "I think our parents could learn from this program!" That was enough to get Hillsdale's Family Literacy Program off the ground.

Maria, an 8-year-old, attended Hillsdale. During the day, she learned to write and type on computers using *Talking Fingers*. During evening classes at the school's computer lab, she helped teach what she learned to her mother, Angelica, who eventually got a data-entry job. She likely would not have gotten that job without help from an unexpected source—her daughter.

Angelica and Maria's new writing skills were the result of the special after-hours Computers for English program offered to Spanish- and Vietnamese-speaking families. According to Phyllis Shedroff, vice principal at the school, about 40% of Hillsdale's students were from families in which English is not spoken in the home. "The wonderful part of this program," Phyllis said, "is that parents learn English skills in a non-threatening place while they're having fun at the computer with their children."

Huong was a teenager in sixth grade. He came in to watch one night. He saw adults and children working side by side at computers consulting with one another, occasionally in Vietnamese. He watched a third-grade boy writing a story about his dog in English, while a girl next to him was typing away at her keyboard in Vietnamese. Her grandmother sat at her own computer and repeated the sounds "f" and "a" as she typed FA FA FA.

Huong saw everyone learning practical computer skills and English, both of which he knew he would need in order to succeed at school and get a good job. After begging the teacher to stay, Huong joined the class and eventually brought three of his teenaged Vietnamese friends.

"They didn't really belong in this class," confessed Pat Parsons, the teacher, "but they were eager to learn and it was better for them to be here than on the street. They got through the whole program and I'm proud of them!"

Classes, held twice a week, started out with conversations. Pat talked about the pictures from *Talking Fingers* that were posted all over the walls. "Tonight we're going to work on the sound 't,'" she would say, pointing to a tiger. "This is a tiger, it starts with the sound 't'—now you say it." Everyone said "tiger" and found the letter T on their practice keyboards. A young Vietnamese interpreter helped them use the word "tiger" in a sentence. Then they went on to a picture of a tent, a top, and a tree, discussing each one and working on their pronunciation. On the computer, when they saw these pictures they typed the letter T, using the correct finger.

"Last year, the computers were just locked up here in the school at night, not doing anyone any good," says Phyllis. "Then we got funding from the Knight and Valley Foundations for teachers and the *Talking Fingers* program, and the results have been spectacular."

Altogether, through several sessions, Vietnamese classes were attended by 31 parents and 78 students. Of the Spanish-speaking families, 113 adults and 51 students attended, many coming to more than one 10-week session. They all spoke English, but needed to improve their reading and writing in English. Two other women besides Angelica left the class because they were able to get data-entry jobs.

Graduation ceremonies were big events. Children and adults alike walked proudly to the front table as their names were called to receive their "diplomas" and get a heartfelt congratulation and handshake from Phyllis, Pat, and the interpreter. The most frequently asked question on the last day was, "When does the next class start?

Chicago, Illinois, 1997

"I think we should do some research with at-risk first graders!"

I had met Dr. Joe Torgesen several times at conferences, but we had never spoken at length. I admired the work he was doing at the University of Florida: He and his colleagues were showing quite clearly how important phoneme awareness and phonics were to skilled reading. I wanted to show him *Read, Write & Type!*, so I emailed him to set up an appointment at the next reading-disabilities conference.

We sat down together in the lobby of the hotel and I explained the ideas behind *Read, Write & Type!*. I showed him the main screen with the keyboard houses and the rest of Sound Town—the Theater, the Park, the Story Tree, and the Hall of Fame—where different activities take place.

"The two houses are a graphic and concrete way to represent the keyboard," I explained. "There's one for each hand. (You keep your left hand in the yellow house.) Once you've got something concrete that children can relate to, you can tell a story about it. The characters who live in these two houses are storytellers and their names start with the sounds where they live, so there's Cass the Cat, Gus the Goose, and so on. They want to get to the Story Tree to write down their stories, but Vexor the Virus doesn't like stories and he tries to steal the letters from the storytellers. Kids love to foil him—he's a grouchy opponent, but very funny and endearing."

Right away, Joe began to catch on. "So the kids want to win for the storytellers!"

"That's right, and those Helping Hand characters can show the correct finger-stroke on the keyboard when students make a mistake, so they get visual as well as auditory feedback to correct any error."

Joe started the program and got to a place where the game asked him to type the word CAT. He deliberately made a mistake and typed S instead of A. The Helping Hand on the left, Lefty La Dee (because she "anchors" to the D key), said "Type 'aaa.'" Her pinky finger changed color and moved to type the A key on the screen.

"Oh, that's nice! I like this, Jeannine. I'd like to look at it more closely. I think we should do some research with at-risk first graders using this program!"

It was just what I was hoping for!

Tallahassee, Florida, 1998

"It's going to be so much fun teaching with this program!"

Joe Torgesen set up a research project in Tallahassee schools. I flew there several times to train the teachers Joe had hired, who were enthusiastic and competent. On the first day I was there, one of them said, "It's going to be so much fun teaching with this program!"

Joe identified the 20% of students most at risk for reading failure at the beginning of first grade. The children were taught in small groups using a combination of teacher-led and computer-assisted instruction in 50-minute sessions, 4 days a week from October through May (for a total of 88 hours). One group received instruction with *Read, Write & Type!* materials, and the other received instruction with the Lindamood *Auditory Discrimination in Depth* program. Here's what Joe wrote about the project:

> *The purpose of the study was to examine the relative effectiveness of two computer-supported approaches to teaching beginning reading skills that differed in important aspects of their instructional approach and emphasis. One of the programs was* Auditory Discrimination in Depth *(ADD), which provides very explicit instruction and practice in acquiring phonological awareness and phonemic decoding skills. In this program, children spend a lot of time practicing word-reading skills out of context, but they also read phonetically controlled text in order to learn how to apply their word-reading skills to passages that convey meaning. This method of instruction is widely used in the United States to help reading-disabled children acquire beginning reading skills. The other program was* Read, Write & Type! *(RWT), which provides explicit instruction and practice in phonological awareness, letter-sound correspondences, and phonemic decoding, but does so primarily in the context of encouraging children to express themselves in written language. In this program, children spend a greater proportion of their time processing meaningful written material, and they are encouraged to acquire "phonics" knowledge to enable written communication.*
>
> *Children were seen from October through May in groups of three children. The children received four 50-minute sessions per week during this time. Approximately half the time in each instructional session was devoted to direct instruc-*

tion by a trained teacher in skills and concepts that would be practiced on the computer. In the RWT condition, this instruction consisted of the "warm-up" activities outlined in the teacher's manual. The remainder of the time was spent with the children working individually on the computer, with the teacher in a support role.

Occasionally, if a particular child was having difficulty with a specific skill, the teacher would provide additional individualized instruction while the other two children in the group were working on the computer. The ADD group received instruction in exactly the same way, except that the nature of the teacher-led activities, as well as the computer-support activities, was different.

Children in both instructional groups showed large gains in relative standing in reading skills from pre to post tests. The only statistically reliable difference in reading gain between the groups occurred on the Nonword Efficiency measure, and the ADD group was stronger on this measure.

The big surprise here was how well everyone did. Particularly in phonemic reading skills, the children in both groups showed very large gains (two full standard deviations) in this area, and their gains in fluency were almost as strong as those for accuracy. The results are encouraging for both intervention programs. It is also important to note that the reading-comprehension scores were higher than expected based on the children's estimated general verbal ability.

Our conclusion is that both the RWT and the ADD curriculum are effective ways to teach early reading skills to children at risk for reading problems. In one sense, it was a bit surprising that the RWT program, which is not as explicit nor intensive in providing instruction and practice in phonological awareness and phonemic reading skills, produced just as much growth in these areas as the ADD program did. In part, this may be because the program was so engaging for the children who worked with it.

First graders who started with phonetic reading skills in the bottom second percentile raised their scores to the 55th percentile. In other words, by the end of first grade, these "at-risk" students in the Read, Write & Type! program had phonetic reading skills that were slightly above grade level.

Tallahassee, Florida, 1998 (continued)

The program was particularly effective in teaching children how to decode, or "sound out," words they had never seen before. It is a novel and interesting way to provide the systematic and explicit instruction in phonics that is being currently advocated by researchers as a way to obtain more balanced and effective instruction in reading. In fact, the Read, Write & Type! *program, in its basic instructional design and content, is entirely consistent with the elements that research has shown to be important to effective reading instruction.*

If the program is used as outlined in the teacher's manual, and children receive the preparatory teacher-led activities and instruction that are described in that manual, our research indicates that the Read, Write & Type! *program can be very helpful with both average and at-risk children in building critical beginning skills in reading and writing. In addition, the children receive the added bonus of learning how to be touch-typists.*

San Rafael, California, 2008

"I've finished! Read, Write & Type! *is ready for Web delivery!"*

Scott is a brilliant programmer and a champion parachutist, but very modest and shy. We were having lunch when Scott came in and quietly announced the completion of 10 months' of work: re-programming *Read, Write & Type!* and its companion CD, *Spaceship Challenge,* in Flash so it could be used on the web.

"I've finished! *Read, Write & Type!* is ready for Web delivery!" He backed away as I jubilantly went up to hug him. "There are a few things left to do, but the hard part is done," he explained.

It was a triumphant moment. Now the program could be delivered to anyone who wanted to learn to read and write in English with voiceover help and Instructions in English, Spanish, Arabic, Malaysian, Mandarin, Farsi, and Japanese (with more languages to come)! Now we wouldn't have to worry about new operating systems and the enormous cost of upgrading for every new system that was released. And we wouldn't have to worry about piracy when we made it available
to other countries.

Now we really had a gift for the world—an effective literacy and touch-typing program for children and adults to play anywhere in the world.

Talking Fingers, our company that developed *Read, Write & Type!,* is very small. Our mindset is that of a nonprofit: We have no stockholders to impress and we are not as interested in the bottom line as we are in helping children learn to read. Our goal is to recoup the costs of development, manage the maintenance of the program on the web, add new languages to the voiceover help, and spread the word that *Read, Write & Type!* is now available for online play.

Is it time to retire? No, there's always more to do! The children with their hungry little brains are out there trying to grow up smart and literate in a world that needs their intelligent participation.

Part 2
How To Teach Children To Construct Words First

This part of the book provides the nuts and bolts you need to lead a child to reading. You don't need any particular materials or products to get started—it's the encoding approach that's important. There are lots of good products available to buy. I have talked about *Read, Write & Type!* in the anecdotes about my life because the research that has been done with it and the experiences we have had with it are helpful for validating the effectiveness of the encoding approach. It is the only software product available that takes this approach in depth. But you can also get started without any specific product to lead a child to reading—just some good sense, paper, and pencils will do.

This section will only deal with the first four doors to literacy: (1) conversation, (2) phoneme awareness, (3) phonics via encoding, and (4) the progression from encoding to decoding to reading and writing. It will show you how to teach the skills children need to be able to automatically segment a word into its sounds and produce the letters that stand for those sounds. Then, as they read back what they have written, they will develop blending and decoding skills for reading.

There is more work to do after they master these first four skills: They will need to know more about how words are built in English and the spelling rules that govern that construction. They will need to develop strategies for tracking the meaning of longer sentences, paragraphs, and stories; for predicting; and for reading fluently. But these come later. Here we are building the foundation: the neural connections that will allow the development of fluent reading to occur within an efficient network of speech, comprehension, and word recognition.

Chapter 8
The First Door to Literacy: Conversation

The first door is conversation because conversation requires both speech and comprehension. Since the foundation of reading is speech, the most important preparation for reading is lots and lots of conversations from the earliest days of a baby's life. Babies' brains are designed to soak up languages and the critical period for this mental nourishment is in the first 3 years of life.

The importance of conversation was discussed at length in Chapter 5. In the first three years, the very young brain develops the early connections that will multiply its capacity for learning. Babies can easily learn one language from a father and another from a mother or caretaker. Every new word enables the child to create a new sentence, request, or question about the world.

Parents should look at their babies when they're talking, and make eye contact. Parents often talk to their babies while they are in strollers. (Or, more often these days, adults talk on cellphones without relating to the baby at all.) But babies need to see the face that's talking. They need to see a face because they are using their mirror neurons to mimic what they see and hear. Parents instinctively mimic back, even if the sounds are meaningless noises.

Each walk or visit to the grocery store is an opportunity for talking. Walking up stairs can become a counting game. Driving in the car can be a time for word games or songs.

Encourage young children to ask questions and answer them thoughtfully. Read stories and discuss the pictures and the story together. These early conversations provide the vocabulary and the knowledge of language structures that prepare a child for reading and for enjoying the process of finding meaning in text. Reading skills will depend on the speech and comprehension skills that underlie them.

Chapter 9

The Second Door to Literacy: Phoneme Awareness

The next thing children need to learn is that when they say a word, their mouths are making several sounds. This is not easy for them to understand, because children are used to thinking of words as whole sounds.

The Second Door and the Third Door should be "entered" at the same time. Recent research in Portugal suggests that children learn phoneme awareness better when the sounds they are learning to identify are actually linked to letters as they learn the alphabet code for those sounds. So the activities suggested in this chapter are mostly games that can be played or sung in the car or standing in line, or riding the bus. Learning to use the code by manipulating letters and encoding are covered by the activities in the next chapter. They will help solidify the awareness of the sounds in words.

Let's imagine that you're teaching a girl named Maria. Say the word PIG and ask Maria to watch your lips. "See how my mouth changes when I say the word?" you ask. "First I put my lips together and pop the air out ('p'). Then my lips smile and I say 'i.' Then I close my throat and pop the air through while my

> **❝**Appropriate activities at the pre-alphabetic level include phonological awareness tasks (carried out orally) such as rhyming; counting, adding and deleting syllables; matching beginning consonants in words; recognizing odd sounds; substituting sounds; and identifying that a sound exists in selected words.**❞**
>
> *Louisa Moats, 1998*

voice makes the sound 'g'." Ask Maria to say the word PIG and watch herself in the mirror so she can see and feel herself making those sounds.

Phoneme awareness comes with playing lots of games—in the car, standing in line at the post office, in the kitchen, or in pre-school. Use that precious time for conversation or games. Here are some games you can play.

Rhymes

Start with rhyming so Maria and Johnny become aware of how different words rhyme when you change the first sound, like BIG and PIG. Do these words rhyme? How about BIG and BAG? They have some of the same sounds, but they don't rhyme. If you play these games, pretty soon children will be able to tell when words sound alike and when they sound different.

Start by reading lots of rhymes and jingles, and singing songs. Repeat nursery rhymes often enough that a child can fill in a rhyming word when you leave it out.

> Jack and Jill went up the _____ (*hill*).

> Mary had a little lamb, its fleece was white as snow
> And everywhere that Mary went, the lamb was sure to _____ (*go*).

Any rhymes that you learned as a child will do. You can even make up new verses:

> Hey diddle diddle, the cat and the fiddle
> The cow jumped over the moon.
> The little dog laughed to see such sport
> And the dish ran away with the ___ (*spoon*).

> Hey diddle diddle, the cat and the fiddle
> The cow jumped over the house.
> The little dog laughed to see such sport
> And the cat ran away with the ___ (*mouse*).

> Hey diddle diddle, the cat and the fiddle
> The cow jumped over the man.
> The little dog laughed to see such sport
> And the pot ran away with the ___ (*pan*).
>
> Hey diddle diddle, the cat and the fiddle
> The cow jumped over the stork.
> The little dog laughed to see such sport
> And the knife ran away with the ___ (*fork*).

You get the idea.

Songs

You can do the same thing with songs. Sing the song until it's familiar, then leave out some of the rhyming words for the child to fill in:

> This old man, he played two, he played knick-knack on my ___ (*shoe*).
> This old man, he played three, he played knick-knack on my ___ (*knee*).
>
> The itsy-bitsy spider went up the water spout.
> Down came the rain and washed the spider ___ (*out*).

Guessing Games

1. What am I Thinking? Don't make this game too hard. (Success is a great motivator!) Make it easy at first, and then give fewer hints as the child gets good at the game. Start out with something like this:

> I'm thinking of a word that rhymes with BIG. It's an animal and it's fat and pink and it says "oink."

2. Playing with Names What would Jack's name sound like if it started with B? (BACK) What if it started with F? (FACK) And so on.

> What about Jane's name? JANE, BANE, FANE, GANE, etc. What about my name? MOMMY, TOMMY, SOMMY, etc.

3. I Spy Find an object in the immediate environment and make up a puzzler like this:

> "I spy with my little eye, something that starts with the sound 'k' and rhymes with GOAT." (*COAT*)

"I spy with my little eye, something that starts with the sound 'wh' and rhymes with STEEL." (*WHEEL*)

"I spy with my little eye, something that starts with the sound 'b' and rhymes with COOK." (*BOOK*)

You can take turns—Maria can try to mystify you with an "I spy" of her own! Play this game with all the consonant sounds and the digraph sounds in the table on page 84. When the child is good at beginning sounds, try switching the game to ending sounds:

"I spy with my little eye, something that ends with the sound 'l' and rhymes with TALL." (*BALL*)

4. Variations Play all these same guessing games with:

- Beginning sounds
- Ending Sounds
- Middle Sounds

5. Say Without This game is a little harder. Start with compound words, like MAILMAN, HIGHWAY, BOXCAR, FOOTBALL, FLASHLIGHT, RAILROAD, AIRPLANE, etc. It goes like this:

You say to Johnny, "Say MAILMAN."
Johnny says, "MAILMAN."
"Now say it without the MAN."
He says "MAIL."
"Now say it without the MAIL."
"MAN."

Here are some other possibilities:

BARNYARD	SIXTEEN	TOLLGATE
SAILBOAT	HEADLIGHT	CARPOOL
BLUEBIRD	DRAWBRIDGE	POLICEMAN
CHILDHOOD	AIRPORT	UNDERWEAR
STOPLIGHT	SUNSET	SUPERMAN
MOTORCYCLE		

When Johnny is good at compound words, try having him leave out a sound at the beginning of a word:

> You say to Johnny, "Say CART."
> He says, "CART."
> You say, "Now say it without the 'k' sound."
> He says, "ART."

When he's good at beginning sounds, try an ending sound:

> You say to Johnny, "Say CART."
> He says, "CART."
> You say, "Now say it without the 't' sound."
> He says, "CAR."

Turn the game around so Johnny can make up one for you to try:

> Try a word where you leave out a sound in the middle:
> "Say PLUMP."
> "Now say it without the 'l' sound."
> He says, "PUMP."
>
> "Say STICK"
> "Now say it without the 't' sound"
> He says, "SICK."
>
> "Say WINTER."
> "Now say it without the 't' sound."
> He says "WINNER."
>
> BRANCH without the "b" (RANCH).
> BRING without the "b" (RING).
> THINK without the "th" (INK).
> DUMP without the "d' (UMP).
> MUST without the "s" (MUT).
> MILK without the "l" (MIK).

You will know Johnny and Maria have mastered phoneme awareness when they can segment any word into its separate sounds and play with the sounds in words.

The 40 Sounds (Phonemes) in English

5 vowels: A, E, I, O, U, (use only the short vowel sounds such as in PAT, PET, PIT, POT, and CUT. Notice I didn't say PUT—that's not the short U sound!)

20 consonant sounds: B, C, D, F, G, H, J, K, L, M, N, P, R, S, T, V, W, X, Y, Z

5 long vowels (the "name sounds" of each vowel as in GATE, ME, HI, NO, CUTE)

5 consonant pairs: TH, SH, CH, WH, NG

3 vowel pairs: OO as in BOOK, OO as in MOON, OU as in OUT

2 consonant-vowel pairs: AW as in HAWK, QU as in QUIT

Add them up and you get 40!

Chapter 10

The Third Door to Literacy: Phonics via Encoding

New light has been shed on the learning of phoneme awareness by the Portuguese psychologist Jose Morais. His research shows that *phoneme awareness comes with learning an alphabetic code.* When Morais compared the performance of illiterates and literates on games requiring awareness of phonemes, he discovered an amazing thing: Although the illiterates were able to distinguish speech sounds such as the difference between "pa" and "da," and could recognize that the words LABEL and TABLE have the same ending, they were unable to do tasks requiring the discrimination of the smallest components of a word—its phonemes. They could not hear that the same phoneme "t" occurred in different places in the words TUNA, STOP or FOOT. They were even unable to substitute a new sound for an existing sound, such as in the game described in the last chapter—your name is Buddy, what would it sound like if it started with the sound "p"? Puddy!

So this chapter will explain how to put phoneme awareness together with the learning of our alphabet code. Let's review some basic principles to keep in mind as you introduce letters:

> **"**Studies by the psychologist Jose Morais have shown that the discovery of phonemes ...requires explicit teaching of an alphabetic code. Even adults, if illiterate, can fail to detect phonemes in words. Illiterates systematically failed whenever a game required attention to be directed to the phoneme level.**"**
>
> *Stanislas Dehaene*

- Words are made of sounds (40 in English).
- Letters stand for those sounds.
- Letter sounds are more useful than letter names.
- It's easier to remember just a few things at a time.
- Introduce only one vowel and a few consonants at first
- Start by spelling out three-letter word families like CAT, HAT, FAT, etc. (Always use real words.)
- Use capital letters because they are easier to write
- Associate the shape of the letter with some object that starts with the sound of the letter and resembles the shape of the letter (like "m" for mountains).

Use Letter Sounds Rather than Letter Names

As children begin to learn that words are made up of individual sounds, they can immediately start learning the letters that represent those sounds. When you introduce letters, it's less confusing if you refer to the letters mostly by the *sounds* they make rather than their names. Here's a puzzler that illustrates this point:

This is a list of some words that first graders have written in their stories. See if you can figure out the words they were trying to write:

1. PPL	2. TST
3. YL	4. LFUNT
5. CL	6. DP
7. NHR	8. JL
9. RM	10. THAQ

How many did you figure out? Did you get them all right? Some are pretty hard!

Answers 1. people, 2. test, 3 while, 4. elephant, 5. seal, 6. deep, 7. nature, 8. jail, 9. arm, 10. thank you

These words reveal the most common spelling error in early writing. What is it? If the answer doesn't come to you immediately, go back and pronounce each word aloud as you look at its spelling. Spend some time listening to yourself say the words. This exercise will help you understand a big problem that first graders have.

The answer most people give is that the children are leaving out vowels. Yes, they are leaving out vowels, and that is a common error at this age. But there's another, more significant error in all the words on the list that reveals a flaw in the way we introduce children to letters: The children are using the letters' *names* instead of the letters' *sounds*. If you didn't come up with this answer, go back and pronounce the words again until you understand how the children were thinking. Here are the letter names they were using: 1-P, 2-S, 3-Y, 4-L, 5-C, 6-D, 7-H, 8-J, 9-R, 10-Q.

Why are they using letter names? Because we *teach* letter names first, starting with the Alphabet Song, and we tell children that it's very important to learn letter names. When children ask us how to spell a word, we spell it out by naming the letters.

We probably use letters names at least ten times more frequently than letter sounds. But which is more useful? We're introducing a code for a language (English) that has 40 sounds. There are 26 letters that we use to represent these sounds. Learning these sound-letter associations is a big job for first graders, but we make it harder than it needs to be because we use the letter *names* so frequently. The vowels are the only letters that *ever* "say" their names—in other words, a sound that is the same as their names. (All vowels also have at least one other sound, called the "short" sound.)

We need a way to refer to each letter, but suppose we referred to each letter as its *sound* rather than its name. Isn't it possible that we could use letter names much less frequently? What children need to learn and use every day is the association between sounds and letters. The names could take a secondary role, so children can learn sound-letter associations fluently without confusion.

Parents start teaching the Alphabet Song when children are about 2 years old; it's a way of naming all the letters in a particular order. But are the names really important for reading or writing? When do you need a letter's name to read or write? And is the order important? Only if you're going to look up words in a dictionary, and surely that comes a bit later.

Suppose that when we show children the letter B, we call it a "b" instead of a B. (Here, lowercase "b" refers to the *sound* of the letter; uppercase B refers to the *name* of the letter). Don't say "buh" because adding the "uh" sound to the "b" can be confusing. After all, we don't say "buh-at" for BAT. Instead, say the sounds for letters like B, D, and G with as short an "uh" as possible. For letters like F and S, you can stretch out the sound: "ffff" and "ssss".

If we refer to letters by their sounds, children will realize immediately that letters are for representing the sounds in words. If they are familiar with the sounds, they won't make the spelling errors represented in the puzzlers above. When they ask us how to write CAT and we reply "Sound it out—'c,' 'a,' 't,'" they get the message from the very beginning that it is the *sounds* in words that are represented by letters.

> **"**It is of little use to tell a child that a word is a string of letters that stand for the sounds in words. If, however, we can have a child see the visible assembly of a word out of letters moving to form that word,... the idea becomes real, real enough for that child to 'make words' in the same manner—piecing them together a letter at a time.**"**
>
> *John Henry Martin*

To draw attention to what the mouth is doing to make a speech sound, have children look in a mirror, or pair up and watch each other make the sound. They should notice the shape of the mouth, how the air comes out, whether the throat is open or closed, and whether the sound "has a voice" or not.

There are pairs of consonants in English that are made with the same mouth movement. One member of the pair has a "voice" and the other does not. The "p" in PIG has no voice, while the "b" in BIG is voiced. Hold your hand lightly over your throat and pronounce "p" and the "b"; you'll feel your throat vibrate when you say "b." Try the same thing with "k" and "g," or "t" and "d," or "ch" and "j")

San Rafael, California, 2015

"We need to start earlier!"

There's no doubt about it. All the research is showing that we need to provide richer learning experiences for our very young children, starting at birth! What could our Talking Fingers team do? We decided to use our Talking Shapes in a new product for four and five year olds.

We applied for our fifth Small Business Innovative Research grant from the National Institute of Child Health and Development and got it. We developed seven apps, called *Talking Shapes* that can be played on any tablet, AND also played as a web-based curriculum on any computer with an added assessment component.

Letters are shapes that talk. They were invented to change the sounds in spoken words into shapes that we can see.

Talking Shapes tells the story of two sisters (long, long ago) who invented the alphabet. Each of the seven apps introduces children to "Talking Shapes" -- letters embedded in pictures that call to mind both the shape and the sounds they represent. Children learn to draw the letters and construct words with them.

 Independent research with *Talking Shapes* was carried out by Dr. Margie Gillis, of LiteracyHow, in East Haven, Connecticut schools. After half a year of using *Talking Shapes*, pre-K students in the treatment groups performed better at the beginning of Kindergarten on DIBELS measures of literacy skills, compared to both students who were in the control group and all other students in the district who were entering kindergarten, indicating that the treatment group was significantly more prepared for kindergarten than all other students.

Teaching Phonics

Once children are able to rhyme words and identify the beginning, middle and ending sounds in words, they can start to learn the letters that stand for those sounds. You can use the Talking Shapes, or—if you have alphabet magnets on the refrigerator or alphabet blocks—you can start to play with letters and use them to construct short words.

> **66** *Children ought to learn how to read by creating their own spellings for familiar words as a beginning....Once they know the letters of the alphabet (sounds, not names) they should spend time putting letters together to make words of their own choosing...It is a great thing to put together a word by figuring out for yourself what comes first, what comes next, and so on until you have the whole word laid out in front of you. And what better way to read for the first time than to try recognizing the very word you have just carefully built up on the table in front of you?* **99**
>
> *Dr. Carol Chomsky*

Teach *one* way to represent the 40 basic phonemes

Since English has so many different ways to represent some sounds, it's important to start with the most common and stick with those until they are well-learned. There is a sequence of letters and words listed on the next page, that starts easy and gradually gets more complicated. This list of 7 levels can become the structure for introducing sounds and letters a few at a time. It is the same sequence that is in the *Talking Shapes* software. The titles in parentheses are the titles of the stories in the seven apps.

Start with the sounds and letters in Level One. Children should not go on to Level Two until they can segment (sound out) and spell most of the Level One words. Once they are able to identify the separate sounds in words and associate letters with those sounds using that limited number of letters and sounds, they will be ready to add a few more phonemes at a time to their repertoire. If they have arrived here, they have mastered a *huge hurdle.* Don't hurry on until they seem to understand the process.

Sequencing Phonics Instruction

Pages of letters for each level are at the back of this book. Cut and use the letters for spelling the key words for each level. Duplicates are included on each page for writing the key words.

LEVEL 1 -- (THE FAT CAT)
New letters/sounds: Long A, F, A, T, C, H, S
Duplicates: S, A, C, H, T
Key Words: A, FAT, CAT, SAT, HAT (Use paper for spaces).

LEVEL 2 – (SILLY HEN)
New letters/sounds: Long E, L, E, N, P, M
Duplicates A, C, H, T, S, E
Key Words: MAN, PAN, CAN, HEN, PEN, PET, SET, LET, HE, ME

LEVEL 3 – (DANCING PIG)
New letters/sounds: Long I, J, W, I, B, G
Duplicates: F, N, T, D, P, H
IF, IN, IT, FIN, BIG, PIG, DIG, JIG, WIG, HI, I

LEVEL 5 – (THE BIG SNEEZE)
New letters/sounds: U, Z, OO, AW
Duplicates: S, M, J, T, C, P, F, N
Key Words: UP, CUP, FUN, SUN, SAW, JAW, PAW, ZOO, TOO, MOON, SOON

LEVEL 6 – (THE PET BET)
New letters/sounds: "Long" Y, WH, Y, V, R
Duplicates: E, U, N, A, T, S, M
Key Words: RUN, RAT, YES, MY, TRY, WHY, WHEN, VAN

LEVEL 7 – (THE ROYAL VISIT)
New letters/sounds: QU, K, NG, OO, OU, TH
Duplicates: T, I, S, CH, E, C
Key Words: KING, SING, THING, OUCH, COUCH, QUIT, TOOK, COOK, THIS, THE

Before you start teaching the letters in the first level, check out the procedures suggested below. The letters in the first two levels will last a few weeks, because if Johnny and Maria get used to building the words that can be made with those 11 letters, they'll be well on their way to reading—*without even finishing the alphabet!*—because they will understand how letters are used to represent sounds. After that hurdle, it's just a matter of adding more sounds and letters. Don't go on to the third level until the sounds and letters in the first two levels are pretty well learned.

Suggested Procedures for the First Three Sessions

Session One

Start out with three letters: C, A, T.

Assemble them together one by one to make the word CAT, saying the sound (not the name!) of each letter as you place it—"c," "a," "t."

Carry on a conversation like this as you play with the letters:

"This is the way to write CAT. Watch me."

Take the letters apart again and scramble them up.

"Let's see, CAT. First I need a 'c.' Do you know which one says 'c'?" If the child doesn't know, pick up the C. You can point out that the cat in the picture is curled around like a C.

"Oh, here it is. I'm going to put it down here. Now, let's see…what's the next sound? CAT. 'c,' 'a.' We need the letter that says 'a.' Do you know which one says 'a'?" If the child doesn't know, pick up the A and place it to the right of the letter C. Point out that the picture of the ACROBAT starts with the sound "a."

"Now we have 'ca.' What's the last sound? Say it with me: CAT." Draw out the "a" as you say it—"caaaaaaa-t"—and emphasize the "t." "Let's see, 't' is for TREE, Do you see a tree? There's the 't'!" Pick up the T and place it to the right of the CA.

"Look! We've made CAT!"

Repeat the process—scrambling the letters and making CAT—until the child starts picking up the right letters. If she finds the right letters, give her lots of praise. ("Wow! In one lesson, you've learned three letters and a word! Next time you'll learn another letter and you can write two words!") *If she seems bored or tired, quit right away and come back to it another time.*

Session Two

Start out with four letters: C, A, T, F.

Begin by assembling the word CAT.

"Remember this one?" Let her answer if she remembers. "It says CAT." Point to each letter and say its sound: "c," "a," "t."

Scramble the letters as you did in Session 1. Ask "Can you remember how to make CAT?" and see if she can find the letters and construct CAT.

"What do you think will happen if I take away the 'c'? If I take away the 'c,' it will say AT." Point to each letter and say the sound ("a," "t"). Then blend them together, saying "aaaaat." You might say a sentence to explain the word AT, like, "Daddy is AT the store."

"See if you can make a new word. If this says AT and this new letter says 'f,' how would you make FAT?" Let's find the picture of the FOX. FOX starts with 'f.' See how he looks like an F when he holds his paw out with the flower?" If she doesn't know, put the F in front of the AT to make FAT and sound it out again, pointing to each letter—"'f,' 'a,' 't'." (She may need several tries).

Be patient. This is *the* major concept underlying reading: understanding that words are made of sounds and that squiggles on paper can stand for sounds. If she has difficulty or gets frustrated, go back to the sound games you were playing in the last chapter, then try this again later.

Review Sessions 1 and 2 until she seems to be catching on.

Session Three

Start out with five letters (C, A, T, F, H) and 2 blanks.

Review CAT and FAT, and then introduce H:

> "If I take away the 'f' and put this letter H in front of AT, it will say HAT. Look for the picture of a hat. The word 'hat' starts with 'h.' You say it when you laugh—ha, ha, ha!"
>
> You can now build AT, FAT, CAT, and HAT. Explain that when A is all by itself, it usually says "uh."
>
> Now you can build A CAT, A HAT, and A FAT CAT!
>
> Don't forget to use the blanks between words! Call them "spaces" and when you construct A CAT, sound out each tile as you assemble them, like this: "'uh,' space, 'c,' 'a,' 't.'"
>
> This is a good time to read *The Cat in the Hat* by Dr. Seuss! When you come to CAT and HAT, let her read the words!

Now you have the general idea of how to present new letters. Here are some things to keep in mind as you proceed.

1. As often as you can, refer to letters by their sounds, not their names.

2. Sound out the words with her until she can do it herself.

3. Don't be rigid about the sequence suggested here. If Maria wants to write something else, help her with it, and then go back to the sequence when you can.

4 Find a balance between reviewing previously learned letters and new letters. The best way to do that is to pick words to construct that use mostly old letters and one new letter.

5. Keep the lessons short (15 minutes is enough). Always stop before she loses interest.

6. Have fun together! And encourage any new writing.

"Outlaw" Words

Unfortunately, there are a number of common words in English that don't follow the rules, which means they are not "encodable" or "decodable." Although there may be reasons they are spelled the way they are, those reasons can be explained to a child later. For now, at the early stages of reading and writing, these words will be encountered occasionally as children are reading or writing. Just tell them this is an "outlaw" word that doesn't follow the rules and this word simply needs to be memorized.

For example, a few "outlaw" words can be learned as soon as they are needed, such as TO, ON, and THE. Common "outlaws" encountered early are words like THE, ONE, ONCE, WAS, TO, DO, ONE, TWO, WERE, GONE, THEY, THERE, MOTHER, and FATHER.

A child may make numerous spelling errors when trying to write. Don't try to correct all of them, because that can be very discouraging and confusing. Pick just one or two to correct together, with the reminder that the correct spelling of an "outlaw" word will just have to be memorized. Then make sure that word is repeated again in the next few lessons until its spelling becomes automatic.

Playing with Rimes

The word "rime" (which is *different* from "rhyme" even though the two words sound the same) refers to the last part of the syllable after the first consonant(s). Every syllable has a rime. For example, ACK is a rime. If you add the onset B, the word becomes BACK. It is the same rime as in TACK or SACK.

You can make almost 500 primary-grade words from the following set of only 33 rimes (compiled by Wylie and Durrel, 1970).

Use these rimes to make words when children are practicing with short vowel sounds:

-at, -ack, -an, -ank, -ap, -ash

-et, -ell, -est
-it, -ick, -ill, -in, -ing, -ink, -ip
-ot, -ock, -op
-ut, -up, -uck, -ug, -ump, -unk

Use these rimes to make words when children are learning about the vowels' "name" sounds:

-ake, -ale, -ame, -ate
-ice, ide, -ine
-oke

Other rimes:

-aw, -ay

These four rimes, which use combinations of vowels or consonants, can be used after all the phonemes above are mastered:

-ail, -ain, -eat, -igh

"As soon as the child knows some of the vowels and consonants, we place before him the big box containing all the vowels and consonants which he knows. The directress pronounces very clearly a word: for example 'mama', and brings out the sound of the 'm' very distinctly, repeating the sounds a number of times. Almost always the little one, with an impulsive movement, seizes an M and places it upon the table. The directress repeats 'ma-ma.' The child selects the A and places it near the M. He then composes the other syllable very easily. But the reading of the word which he has composed is not so easy. Indeed, he generally succeeds in reading it only after a certain effort. In this case I help the child, urging him to read and read the word with him once or twice, always pronouncing very distinctly, 'mama, mama.' But once he has understood the mechanism of the game, the child goes forward by himself and becomes intensely interested. We may pronounce any word, taking care only that the child understands separately the letters of which it is composed. He composes the new word, placing one after another, the signs according to the sounds."

Maria Montessori

Chapter 11

The Fourth Door to Literacy: From Encoding to Decoding to Reading and Writing

nce phoneme awareness is developing and children understand that letters stand for the sounds in words, it becomes much easier to decode (read) words. Children should learn first to decode the words they write themselves. They can be encouraged to read what they have written to anyone around—grandparents, parents, siblings, or friends. Let young writers know how pleased you are with their efforts by posting words, sentences, and stories they have written up on the wall.

Using the specific tips in the previous chapter, you can get children started encoding and decoding words with just materials you have available at home. You can use the Talking Shapes from this book. Start with three-letter words. If they have trouble pronouncing the sounds of each letter and blending them together, help them with the words they write, saying, "Remember the sound that letter makes? Say it, and then say the sound of the next letter until you can string them all together to say the word."

❝Your child will first encounter reading when he reads back the words that have been 'talked' onto the paper. This leads directly to the idea that words on paper are no more than thoughts written down, spoken words that can be seen. Thus as children learn how to write what they can say, they also learn to read what they have written, and they understand that these two processes are interrelated.❞

John Henry Martin

They can make up their own sentences to write. Then it's on to reading their own sentences!

There are wonderful decodable books you can read together—they are usually organized together in the library. When you come to a word they have written before, let them sound it out and read it!

Soon, they will be reading and sounding out new words independently. It may come as quite a revelation: "I can read!" Just make sure they are reading mostly words with the sounds and letters they have already learned and have used in writing words. If the material has too many letters they have not already mastered, or the words are irregularly spelled, they may get discouraged. Always stop before they get tired of the activity.

As children gain command of the alphabet code, they will want to write more and more. With their natural urge to express themselves, children will delight in writing things for you to read. They will not be inhibited about trying to spell out anything they can say. It's all right if they misspell a few words in the beginning. Show them that you can read what they write—that's the whole purpose of their attempt to communicate on paper. You can correct their spelling little

❝The mastery of reading lies, above all, in our ability to decode new words. 'Self-teaching' is an essential ingredient on the road to independent reading. Once they master the spelling-to-sound correspondences, children can, on their own, decipher the pronunciations of a novel string and associate it with a familiar meaning. With self-teaching, the neuronal links from letter strings to sound and meaning can be progressively automatized without any further instruction.❞

Stanislas Dehaene

by little and they will also correct themselves as they encounter the same words in books. They will love watching you write notes, or lists, or short rhymes for them. They can dictate letters for you to write until they can write themselves. And they will enjoy reading them to you!

I made a ovrhedpjektr

Me and my sistr
made a ovrhdprjectr.
I mad it with a big box
and a litll box and a mere
and a magnafire and a flashlite.
When the flashlite shines
thruwe the magnafire
and then it shines
on the mere and it bountsis
off the mere and it shines on the wall.
And we made a play.
Jonathan, Age 6

Kacey's Story

Plants grow from a seed and roots.
We grow from food and water and love.
Anamas grow from food and water.
Love grows from fathe.

Drowings grow from a pencel or cran or makr.
A brane grows from lrning.
A stoey grows from an idea
Kacey, First Grade

Encourage this phonetic spelling because each time children make the association between a sound and a letter, those brain pathways are getting more and more automatic.

However, the issue of spelling soon becomes important. Correcting a child's spelling must be done delicately, gradually, and diplomatically. Pick one or two words from a story to "conform to English conventions." If they are told that many words are spelled "wrong" they may get discouraged and lose that wonderful uninhibited exuberance.

Explain that English came from many languages, and at first people spelled things any old way. Then when more people were reading newspapers and books it became important to be more consistent about spelling. So people made up rules about spelling. Most words follow the rules and children can learn about them gradually. Explain that some words in English just have to be learned because they don't follow spelling rules. You can call these words "outlaw words."

The first easy rule should be about the "silent e" on the end of a word that makes the vowels "say their own names." As soon as they learn this rule, they can spell many words like MAKE, HOME, KITE, CUTE, etc. In the story above, Jonathan has obviously learned this rule because he has used it in MADE, SHINES, and FLASHLITE. He tried to use it in MERE, because he probably pronounced the word that way.

Parents and teachers should recognize phonetic spelling for the miracle that it is. It means that children have "got it"—they are mapping sound-letter associations consistently into their brains. Rejoice! Celebrate with smiles and hugs! You can avoid the words "wrong" and "right" and just say something like "this is the way people decided that word should be spelled."

This book is about preparing the brain for reading. By now, it should be clear that encoding is what leads the way to skilled reading and writing—the power of literacy. And this early encoding should be followed by ubiquitous writing at home and at school in every class—lists, notes, science reports, poems, jokes, stories, etc.

> "The major reservation to allowing invented or phonetic spelling is the concern that the spellings are often incorrect. The printed word 'belongs' to the spontaneous speller far more directly than to children who have experienced it only ready made. For once you have invented your own spelling system, dealing with the standard system comes easy. A considerable amount of intellectual work has already been done."
>
> *Dr. Carol Chomsky*

> "Writing—the art of communicating thoughts to the mind, through the eye—is the great invention of the world. Great in the astonishing range of analysis and combination which necessarily underlies the most crude and general conception of it—great, very great in enabling us to converse with the dead, the absent, and the unborn, at all distances of time and space; and great not only in its direct benefits but greatest help to all other inventions."
>
> *Abraham Lincoln*

Chapter 12
Change is Happening

We have arrived a time of great and rapid change in the world. Science has opened up amazing new vistas into the functioning of the human brain. We know much more now about how a child's early experiences actually contribute to the way the brain gets organized—for language and communication; for literacy; for physical, emotional, and social skills; and ultimately for the intelligence needed to make a reasonable living, raise a family, and contribute to a democratic society. Although genetics play a part, the nurturing adults in a child's life are largely responsible for this brain development.

As a society stretching to evolve in ways that will insure a better future for our families, companions, and planet, we need to turn our priorities to our young and invest our financial resources, time, energies, and love in the children of our tribe.

It may be a bit scary to think that, when you teach young children something, you're actually changing their brains, but it's true. We are all changing our brains all the time, especially when we learn something new. It just happens that—for a major, fundamental skill like reading—those brain changes can be efficient or not-so-efficient, depending on how you choose to teach that important skill.

This book has outlined a speech-to-print approach to learning phoneme awareness and phonics, which is a departure from traditional methods. As you think about whether it seems reasonable to you to put decoding and reading on hold for a few weeks to give a child a chance to learn to construct his own words, consider what might be lost and what might be gained.

Some might say that it is a shame for children not to be able to read fine literature right away. But there are hundreds of well-loved children's books to read to them every day. They can enjoy them fully with you, especially if you ask questions, comment, and converse about the books. They will not be deprived of this literature. If you postpone teaching them how to read these books for a short period while they learn to use the alphabet code, they will be better prepared to read them when the time comes.

It seems that nothing is really lost by adopting this strategy, whereas what might be *gained* is multifold: fluency with the alphabet code, a brain organized more efficiently for reading, possible prevention of reading difficulties, skills with writing as well as reading, the confidence and self-esteem that comes with success, and a great deal of joy sharing this process with a child.

Teachers and publishers are becoming more aware of the importance of encoding, and the tide is turning toward including more encoding instruction in schools. In 1997, a seven-year longitudinal study of two different methods of delivering early reading instruction carried out with students in Clackmannanshire, Scotland, sent reverberations through the British educational community. The study found that Scottish children at Primary 7 were reading words *three and a half years* ahead of chronological age when taught with an approach called "synthetic phonics," which includes a heavy dose of encoding. This was far ahead of their British counterparts. Boys were doing as well or better than girls. After a lengthy review, the U.K. National Literacy Strategy advocated changing from "analytic" reading instruction to "synthetic phonics," causing much debate in some circles.

> *The purpose of writing is to convey meaning. The purpose of reading is to reconstruct and consider that meaning.*
>
> *Marilyn Adams*

In America, a similar shift and debate occurred when research showed that "explicit systematic instruction" in phonics improved reading significantly more than Whole Language teaching. Although instruction changed in the U.S. to implement these findings, explicit systematic instruction still doesn't include much encoding. By contrast, the synthetic phonics used in Scotland and England involves much more of the encoding approach described in this book— teaching letter sounds before letter names, and including more segmenting, phoneme manipulation, and writing to dictation. Scottish and British students have improved their reading dramatically.

So change is happening in the U.K., and is beginning to happen in U.S. schools, too. The challenge now is to teachers, parents, and caretakers who may be the first to introduce children to reading. Happily, it's easy to meet that challenge, and hopefully the ideas in this book will help you.

Writing is one of the most challenging, demanding, and satisfying skills we humans master, and it should occupy at least half of language-arts time throughout every grade level in school and be encouraged frequently at home. Writing should be given as much emphasis as reading, but unfortunately, the value of writing has been greatly underestimated by elementary educators as an essential part of literacy.

Writing is a way to learn how to think. As E.M. Forester once said, "How can I know what I think until I see what I say?" As children put their ideas on paper, they have to figure out what they know, what they believe, and what they feel. As they read what they write, the ideas are changed and perfected. The earlier they start learning this process, the earlier they will develop their ability to express ideas clearly and thoughtfully.

Writing came before reading when it was first invented. And writing comes before reading as a natural way to begin to understand words on paper. The writer creates words for the reader to read. It is the writer who initiates the action— who chooses the words, generates the ideas, and actively shapes the meaning of the message. It is the writer who sees the "big picture" but who, at the same time, must assemble the whole message, one piece at a time, from individual sounds and letters. Children can read without writing, but they cannot write without reading.

Children learn best by putting their ideas about the world into their own words and by telling (or writing) about them. Getting feedback from an audience is a good way to learn whether or not their ideas make sense.

San Rafael, California, 2018

"Are you going to retire now, Jeannine?"

Wow--there's a scary question! Am I finished? The emotional fire for my career was kindled in Mississippi with that Head Start Project in 1965. I decided then that I wanted to help kids learn to read. That fire has not gone out. I have spent most of my life developing software that provides evidence-based literacy instruction for preK -3rd Grade students. As of this writing, Read, Write & Type has been used by more than half a million students, in all states and all provinces and in 30 countries. Talking Shapes apps are on the way as well. But when I was asked about retirement, I asked myself, "What could I do with this software now that would make the biggest impact?"

My mission is to empower generations to come with literacy skills. I decided to go back to Mississippi and give away the software to schools and agencies like United Way and Americorps and HeadStart that are really trying to make a difference in literacy in Mississippi, where in some of the poorer counties more than 30% of the population is unable to read or write.

In the last few months I have set up ten sites that have computers and our software, and trained about eighty teachers and volunteers who will set up the programs at their own sites. These sites will use the software during the school year, but also provide summer programs for family literacy and help for struggling students. By summer of this year (2018) I hope to have 20 sites. By 2019, I hope to have at least 60 sites. Americorps (America Reads) is training volunteers that can manage the summer projects. By 2020 I hope to have at least 100 sites, and several hundred trained volunteers. My dream is to have a LITERACY SUMMER IN 2020 and provide instruction for at least 20,000 new readers and writers.

In 1964 we had a FREEDOM SUMMER in Mississippi. We needed to register people to vote, and raise consciousness about voting—so that people would understand that voting is an important CIVIL RIGHT-- and we had a CIVIL RIGHTS REVOLUTION! Now, with two-thirds of American students not reading at grade level, we need the whole country to understand that LITERACY IS A CIVIL RIGHT.

It's time for a LITERACY REVOLUTION!

Acknowledgements

would like to thank the pioneers whose insights charted the course for this book. It was Maria Montessori who first spoke strongly about the importance of constructing words before trying to read them. Romalda Spalding, in her book *The Writing Road to Reading*, outlined very sensible methods for teaching writing and spelling as a vital route to reading. Others have joined the chorus along the way, emphasizing the fundamental role of speech in becoming aware of the sounds in words—Carol Chomsky, Patricia Lindamood, Marilyn Adams, and Louisa Moats. Both scientists and popular writers like Rudolph Flesch (*Why Johnny Can't Read*) and John Henry Martin (*Writing to Read*) have sounded the alarm about the fact that reading instruction must change. I am grateful for their insights and courage.

I would also like to toast Reid Lyon, who, more than anyone else, has been instrumental at the federal level in turning around this unwieldy ship of reading instruction from the fad of Whole Language to systematic phonics, managing the funding and communicating the research showing that phoneme awareness and phonics are essential elements of reading.

I also raise my glass to those who ushered me into the world of neuroscience research—Robert Ornstein, David Galin, Chuck Yingling, and especially Larry Pinneo, who tried to teach me the essentials of writing as he suffered through the preparation of my Ph.D. dissertation. I am also grateful to teachers like Margaret Rechif, who guided me in the ways of the classroom, and to my mentors in software development—Joyce Hakansson, Don Daglow, and Leslie Grimm.

Those who have helped in the preparation of this book—Kris Kuebler and Adam Titone (my colleagues at Talking Fingers); Marcia Friedman (book designer extraordinaire); Dawn Mann (eagle-eyed editor and proofreader); and Mitchell Rose (artist and imaginative creator of Talking Shapes), have my undying gratitude for their assistance and their patience. Lastly, I would like to thank my husband Matt, whose ideas have inspired me for 60 years, and whose writing skills have been an immense help in shaping this book.

Jeannine Herron,
San Rafael, California

References and Resources

Adams, M.J. (1994) *Beginning to Read,* Cambridge, MA: MIT Press.

Aylward, E.H. et al. (2003) "Instructional treatment associated with changes in brain activation in children with dyslexia." *Neurology* 61: 212 – 219.

Chall, J. et al. (1990) *The Reading Crisis,* Cambridge, MA: Harvard University Press.

Chomsky, C. (1971) *Childhood Education* March 1971, Association for Childhood Education International, Washington DC, 296 – 299.

Dehaene, S., (2010) *Reading in the Brain,* London: Penguin Books.

Diamond, M. & Hopson, J. (1999) *Magic Trees of the Mind.* Penguin Group.

Dickinson, E. (1976) *The Complete Poems of Emily Dickinson.* Johnson, T.H. (ed.), New York, Little, Brown & Co.

Ehri, L. (2002) "Phases of acquisition in learning to read words and implications for teaching." *British Journal of Educational Psychology Monograph,* Series II, Number 1, Learning and Teaching Reading: 1 (1): 7 – 28.

Ehri, L. (2004) "Teaching phonemic awareness and phonics." In *The Voice of Evidence in Reading Research,* P. McCardle & V. Chhabra (eds.). (153 – 186) Baltimore: Paul Brookes.

Farnham-Diggory, S. (1986) *Introduction to The Writing Road to Reading.* Romalda Spalding, New York: Wm. Morrow & Co.

Flesch, R. (1955) *Why Johnny Can't Read.* New York: Harper & Row.

Foorman, B.R., et al. (1998) "The role of instruction in learning to read: Preventing reading failure in at-risk children." *Journal of Educational Psychology,* 90: 37 – 55.

Gentry, J.R. (2007) *Breakthrough in Beginning Reading and Writing*, NY, NY: Scholastic, Inc.

Gillingham, A. et al. (1997) *Gillingham Manual: Remedial Training for Children with Specific Disability in Reading, Spelling and Penmanship.* Cambridge, MA: Educators Publishing Service

Gopnik, A. et a. (1999) *The Scientist in the Crib.* New York: Wm. Morrow & Co.

Hall, S. & Moats, L. (1998) *Straight Talk About Reading.* New York: McGraw-Hill.

Hart, B. & Risley, T.R. (2003) *Meaningful Differences in the Everyday Lives of Young American Children.* Baltimore: Paul Brookes.

Henry, M.K., (2003) *Unlocking Literacy.* Baltimore: Paul Brookes.

Kilpatrick, David A. (2015 *Essentials of Assessing, Preventing, and Overcoming Reading Difficulties*, Hoboken, N.J: John Wiley & Sons, Inc.

Martin, J.H. & Freidberg, A. (1986) *Writing to Read.* IBM Corporation.

McCardle, P. & Chhabra, V. (2004) *The Voice of Evidence in Reading Research*, Baltimore, MD: Paul H. Brookes Publishing

Moats, L. (1998 Spring/Summer) "Teaching decoding." *American Educator,* 42 – 49: 95 – 96.

Moats, L. (2000) *Speech to Print,* Baltimore: Paul Brookes.

Orton, S. T. (1989) *Reading, Writing, and Speech Problems in Children.* Baltimore: International Dyslexia Association.

Piaget, J. (1992) "Some aspects of operations." In M. Piers (ed) *Play and Development.* New York.

Pinker. S. (2007) *The Stuff of Thought.* London: Penguin Books.

Rico, G.L. (1983) *Writing the Natural Way.* Los Angeles: J.P Tarcher, Inc.

Seidenberg, M. (2017) *Language at the Speed of Sight*, NY, NY: Basic Books

Shaywitz, S. (2003) *Overcoming Dyslexia: A new and complete science-based program for reading problems at any level.* New York: Knopf.

Simos, P.G. et al. (2002) "Dyslexia-specific brain activation profile becomes normal following successful remedial reading." *Neurology,* 58: 1203 – 1213.

Spalding R.B. (1986) *The Writing Road to Reading.* New York: Wm. Morrow.

Sweet, R.W., Jr. (2004) "The big picture: Where we are nationally on the reading front and how we got here," in *The Voice of Evidence in Reading Research,* Peggy McCardle and Vinita Chhabra (eds). Baltimore: Paul Brookes.

Torgesen, J.K. et al. (2009) "Computer-assisted instruction to prevent early reading difficulties in students at risk for dyslexia: Outcomes from two instructional approaches," in *Annals of Dyslexia.* International Dyslexia Association.

Wolf, M. (2007) *Proust and the Squid.* New York: HarperColllins.

Wolf, M. (2016) *Tales of Literacy from the 21st Century*, Oxford, UK: Oxford University Press

Index

About the author

Jeannine Herron is a research neuropsychologist who became interested in reading-related research in 1965 when she became co-founder and program director of the Child Development Group of Mississippi—a Head Start project serving 5,000 children. She received her PhD. from Tulane Medical School, and went on to do extensive neuroscience research in brain organization and dyslexia at the University of California San Francisco. She edited a book—*Neuropsychology of Lefthandedness*—and has published peer-reviewed papers in *Science, Brain and Language, Journal of Electro-encephalography, Journal of Learning Disabilities, Neuropsychologia, International Journal of Neuroscience,* and a feature article in *Psychology Today.* Jeannine has been a contributing editor for *Science* and *Brain and Language,* has lectured widely and has given many in-service workshops for teachers. She founded California Neuropsychology Services (a non-profit for research in education) in 1982, and Talking Fingers, Inc., (a for-profit for the development of educational products) in 1994, and continues to direct both organizations.

In l970, Jeannine and her family—husband Matt, Matthew (age13) and Melissa (age 11)—sailed a thirty-foot sloop from New Orleans to West Africa and spent a year and a half visiting countries from Mauretania to Ghana, including a 300 mile trip inland up the Gambia River. It was an experiment in alternative education for the children who read more than 100 books, learned some French, studied math from programmed texts, studied marine biology and navigation, absorbed geography and African culture, learned to type, and kept a daily written log of their thoughts and experiences. All four members of the family were authors of *The Voyage of Aquarius*, published by EP Dutton in l974. Talking Fingers has recently published Matthew's log of the African part of the trip in a book with numerous photographs for 9 – 13 year olds called *Our Big Blue Schoolhouse.*

More recently Jeannine has designed, developed, and researched early reading and spelling software (*Read, Write & Type!* and *Wordy Qwerty*) with three grants from the National Institute of Child Health and Human Development (NICHD). Another grant from NICHD funded a collaboration on a product called *SmartCycle,* licensed to Fisher-Price, which became their "Toy of the Year" in 2008. The *Talking Shapes,* featured in this book, are part of seven apps, also funded by NICHD, called Talking Shapes that are available for tablets and also available as a web-based supplement curriculum from the Talking Fingers web site, www.talkingfingers.com.

HELPFUL INSTRUCTIONAL AIDS

The tiles on the following pages can be used as a movable alphabet for children to use as they practice sounding-out and spelling the key words in the seven levels of the Phonics Sequence. (You are not limited to the key words—after you reach Level 2, there are many more words that you and the children can think of using the letters they have learned). I would suggest using the Talking Shapes colored tiles on the last pages first (when children are first introduced to the Phonics Sequence). The Talking Shapes will help children remember the sound and shape of the letters. Once children have made the sound-letter link, they can use the black and white tiles without needing the help of the pictures. Moving from easy-to-harder like this is called "scaffolding." You can find further instructions in Chapter 10.

Each of the seven pages provides the letters you need for each of the seven Levels. (These are the same Levels used in the Talking Shapes software). Duplicates are included on each page for assembling the key words in that Level. You can copy these pages as many times as you like, laminate them for longer use, and cut them up into sets. The following link will give you an idea about how to use them.

https://www.youtube.com/watch?v=O__Hi0LzzTc&list=PL9LqoNGI4ByJF99k8rnul PTqFm_xtfhLC

MATERIALS FOR SEQUENCING PHONICS INSTRUCTION

LEVEL 1 -- (THE FAT CAT)
New letters/sounds: Long A, F, A, T, C, H, S
Duplicates: S, A, C, H, T
Key Words: A, FAT, CAT, SAT, HAT

LEVEL 2 – (SILLY HEN)
New letters/sounds: Long E, L, E, N, P, M
Duplicates A, C, H, T, S, E
Key Words: MAN, PAN, CAN, HEN, PEN, PET, SET, LET, HE, ME

LEVEL 3 – (DANCING PIG)
New letters/sounds: Long I, J, W, I, B, G
Duplicates: F, N, T, D, P, H
IF, IN, IT, FIN, BIG, PIG, DIG, JIG, WIG, HI, I

LEVEL 5 – (THE BIG SNEEZE)
New letters/sounds: U, Z, OO (as in MOON), AW
Duplicates: S, M, J, T, C, P, F, N
Key Words: UP, CUP, FUN, SUN, SAW, JAW, PAW, ZOO, TOO, MOON,
SOON

LEVEL 6 – (THE PET BET)
New letters/sounds: "Long" Y, WH, Y, V, R
Duplicates: E, U, N, A, T, S, M
Key Words: RUN, RAT, YES, MY, TRY, WHY, WHEN, VAN

LEVEL 7 – (THE ROYAL VISIT)
New letters/sounds: QU, K, NG, OO (as in BOOK), OU, TH
Duplicates: T, I, S, CH, E, C
Key Words: KING, SING, THING, OUCH, COUCH, QUIT, TOOK, COOK,
THIS, THE

A	C	S
H	F	T
A	C	S
H	**A**	**T**

Level 2

L	E	N
M	P	A
C	E	H
S	T	E

I	G	B
D	J	W
N	T	F
H	I	P

F	O	X
B	P	I
A	SH	CH
D	G	O

U	C	F
N	Z	P
OO	AW	S
M	J	T

R	Y	E
WH	V	S
U	N	A
M	Y	T

QU	K	NG
OO	OU	TH
T	I	S
CH	E	C

SNAKE	CAT	ACROBAT
TREE	FOX	HAT
SNAKE	CAT	ACROBAT
TREE	Long "A"	HAT

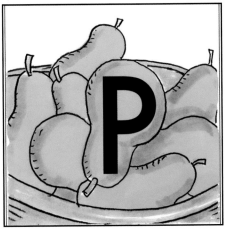

NOODLE	ELEPHANT	LEG
ACROBAT	PEAR	MOUNTAIN
HAT	ELEPHANT	CAT
Long "E"	TREE	SNAKE

 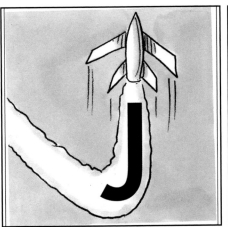 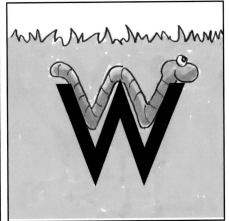

 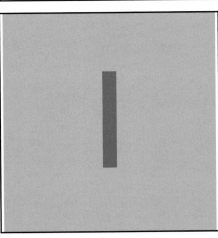 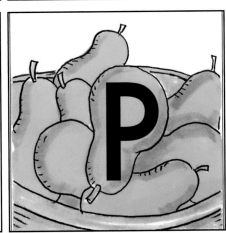

BUTTERFLY	GIRL	INCHWORM
WORM	JET	DOG
FOX	TREE	NOODLE
PEAR	Long "I"	HAT

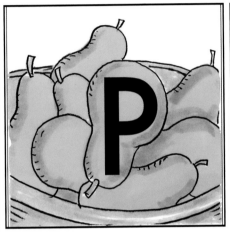

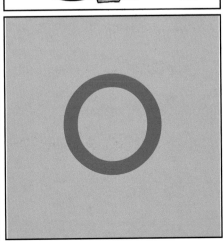

BOX	OCTOPUS	FOX
INCHWORM	PEAR	BUTTERFLY
CHAIN	SHIP	ACROBAT
Long "O"	GIRL	DOG

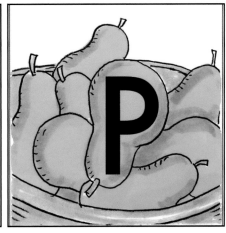

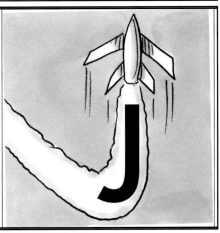

FOX	CAT	UMBRELLA
PEAR	ZIG ZAG	NOODLE
SNAKE	SAW	"OO" as in Moon
TREE	JET	MOUNTAIN

ELEPHANT	YAK	ROOSTER
SNAKE	VALLEY	WHALE
ACROBAT	NOODLE	UMBRELLA
TREE	Long "Y"	MOUNTAIN

WING	KICK	QUILT
THRONE	OUCH	"OO" as in LOOK
SNAKE	INCHWORM	TREE
CAT	ELEPHANT	CHAIN